SURVIVING YOUR CHILD'S
DATING YEARS

SURVIVING YOUR CHILD'S DATING YEARS

7 VITAL SKILLS THAT HELP YOUR CHILD BUILD HEALTHY RELATIONSHIPS

Bobbie Reed, Ph.D.

SAINT LOUIS

With love to Jennifer Reed, who will
someday be teaching her children (my
grandchildren), Spencer, Nicole, Josef, and
Jacob about dating.

Copyright © 1995 Concordia Publishing House
3558 S. Jefferson Avenue, St. Louis, MO 63118-3968
Manufactured in the United States of America

Library of Congress Cataloging-in-Publication Data

Reed, Bobbie.
    Surviving your child's dating years / Bobbie Reed.
        p.   cm.
    Includes bibliographical references.
    ISBN 0-570-04826-5
    1. Dating (Social customs) 2. Interpersonal relations in children. 3. Child
rearing.   4. Dating (Social customs)—Religious aspects—Christianity.
I. Title. II. Series.
    HQ801.R3   1995
    649´.1—dc20   95-7305

1 2 3 4 5 6 7 8 9 10   04 03 02 01 00 99 98 97 96 95

CONTENTS

Introduction: Are Your Kids Ready to Date?   7

1: What Have You Already Taught Them?   11

By your example ... By your manners ... By your mouth ... What's the answer?

2: What Is a *Date*?   25

Casual meetings ... Formal events ... Group events ... Double dating ... Dating alone ... Going steady ... Engaged ... Discuss and agree on definitions

3: How Well Do They Communicate?   34

Teaching kids to speak up ... Teaching kids to ask for what they want ... Teaching kids to refuse unreasonable requests ... Why kids need to learn to communicate effectively

4: Do They Have Good Relational Skills?   62

Teaching kids to accept differences ... Teaching kids to handle confrontation productively ... Teaching kids to build positive relationships

5: Are They Ready for the Dynamics?   84

*Telephoning the opposite sex ... Asking for a date ...
Planning special dates ... Breaking up ... Dealing
with rejection ... Dating ethics*

6: What Are the Dating Rules?   99

*Attraction develops quickly ... Everyone is vulnerable
... Time alone together can be dangerous ... Setting
standards is essential ... Being accountable*

7: Why Wait for Sexual Intimacy?   115

*Reasons kids have sex ... Reasons for kids not to have
sex ... When kids don't wait*

8: What Is the Goal of Dating?   135

*Dating is for learning about relationships ... Dating is
for exploring one special relationship ... Dating myths*

Appendix: Selected Bibliography   144

INTRODUCTION

Are Your Kids Ready to Date?

"I don't know if my kids think they're ready to date,"
Christine confessed, "but I'm not ready for them to start!"

I know what you mean, Christine. Kids grow up fast. The years fly by. Although it seems like only yesterday that they were in diapers, today they are asking if they can go out on a date. For many parents, no matter when that question comes, it comes too early.

Teenage dating is one of the transitions your kids will go through on their journey to adulthood. For some parents, seeing their children exhibit an interest in the opposite sex is "cute" and "interesting." For others, the thought of their teens dating is scary and threatening.

As your children enter the developmental stages we associate with the teenage years, they will experience many changes: physiological, psychological, emotional, social, and intellectual. Dating and sexual awareness are a part of that constant developmental process. Many teenage girls, even the pretty ones, may suddenly discover that they don't feel good about themselves unless a boy thinks they are attractive. Both boys and girls may develop an unusual sensitivity to their physical bodies. Complexion problems, less-than-"perfect" figures, height issues (too short or too tall), irregular teeth, and weight problems become disasters to agonize over as approval from the opposite sex becomes critical.

This book addresses what you can do to prepare your kids for dating. The preparation actually begins long before the first date. Many of the skills required for successful dating relationships are learned early in life, long before there is even an interest in the opposite sex. Starting the learning process early helps your kids prepare for the unique relational challenges of dating.

Your own example is the best way to teach your kids, not only by what you tell them but also by your actions. Teach them to be independent. Teach them to formulate convictions based on biblical principles and God's ideals. Teach them to be ready to stand on those convictions in the face of peer pressure. Encourage your children to be examples of believers, exhibiting the power of God in their lives (1 Tim. 4:12).

Teach your children early in life to speak up for what they believe and to resist the temptation to go along with the crowd. These skills will be invaluable in the dating process. Remember Daniel who stood up to the king for his beliefs? He was only a young man, but God blessed his choice (Dan. 1:3–21). An equally important skill is learning to refuse unreasonable requests and demands or those that conflict with personal convictions. Many adults who failed to learn this skill when they were young find they have become people-pleasers, afraid and unable to set reasonable limits.

You and your kids can work together to set rules that establish acceptable behaviors and limits for their dating relationships. These rules can facilitate conversation, communication, and sharing and protect your teens from becoming overly involved physically. Discussing dating dynamics before your kids are emotionally involved will help them through the awkwardness of new roles and the pain of rejection.

Most young people do not have a deep understanding of the reasons to wait for sexual involvement until marriage. Society accepts sexual activity, even from teenagers, as long as it is "responsible." The world's definition of *responsible* is protection from diseases and unwanted pregnancies for one's self and one's partner. Christians believe premarital sexual activity is against God's standards. However, only a few teens will refrain from giving in to the pressure or the temptation to have sex just because the Bible says it is wrong. They want more information. This book will give you some answers. You'll find more helpful information in the bibliography at the back of this book.

Remember, the goal of dating is to help teens learn—about themselves, about how relationships work, about developing a special relationship with one person, and about developing many types of intimacy, not just physical intimacy. When you understand these goals, you are ready to help your child prepare for dating.

This book is written for parents of preteens, but it will also be helpful for parents of teens who have already started dating.

Have fun!

1
WHAT HAVE YOU ALREADY TAUGHT THEM?

Peter was sharing with a friend about his 16-year-old son's first formal date. "After he picked up his date, they came back to the house for us to take pictures. They were all dressed up and looked terrific.

"His date and Joan, my wife, were talking afterwards. Suddenly, my son became impatient and irritated. 'Come on, come on,' he said harshly. 'We're going to be late!' I was embarrassed at his discourteous behavior.

"Then it dawned on me. I've probably said the same thing in the same way to my wife hundreds of times because she never seems to be in a hurry or to care if we arrive somewhere on time or not. I realized, much to my dismay, that my son had learned his impatient behavior from me!"

Whether you realize it or not, you've already taught your kids a lot about how to relate to the opposite sex in an intimate relationship. The question is, what have you taught them? What have they learned so far? Is it what you would have planned to teach them if you had thought it through beforehand? Perhaps. Perhaps not. Most of us are not on our best behavior at home. Sometimes we treat those we love in ways we would never treat our friends or even casual acquaintances.

If your children are still a few years away from dating, you have plenty of time to choose what you want to teach them about dating and relating to the opposite sex. If your children are already dating or ready to begin dating, it is not too late to change the message you are living at home. More importantly, it's not too late to talk with your kids and share how you believe people should relate to one another.

Remember, your children learn about relationships in your home by listening to you and observing what you do. As parents, you are teaching your kids daily, by your example, by your manners, and by your mouth.

By Your Example

Peter had talked to his kids about being polite and kind to each other (Eph. 4:32) since they were very small. When his son copied his behavior, Peter was reminded that children learn more from watching parental behavior than from listening to parental words.

Children learn what is acceptable behavior from watching you

Children formulate ideas about acceptable behavior by watching how you and your spouse treat each other. Have your children seen you criticize your spouse, use sarcasm, yell at or hit him or her? If so, some part of them will believe that such behaviors are acceptable.

Children who observe such behaviors often vow never to treat their future spouses in the same ways. But it is a proven fact that under stressful conditions, adults tend to revert to behaviors they observed when they were growing up, whether or not they personally approved of them. Therefore, a child who saw parents hitting one another often resorts to hitting when angry or out of control as an adult. A child raised around yelling adults tends to yell a lot as an adult.

Assess your relationship with your spouse and consider it as the example your kids will most likely copy as they mature. Is it the model that you want for your children? If not, talk with your spouse and work together to make changes in your relationship.

Children learn how to deal with conflict from watching you

People deal with conflict and anger in different ways.

- Betty hates disagreements. She *withdraws* at the first sign of an argument. She refuses to present her own ideas, acknowledge her desires, or explain her viewpoint. She leaves the room, takes a walk around the block, or if it is evening, just goes to bed. Betty's needs or desires are rarely met unless they happen to coincide with someone else's needs or desires. Because of how she deals with conflict, Betty is often victimized and taken advantage of by others. Underneath her quiet facade, resentment simmers.

- John approaches conflict to *win* at all costs. He is forceful and aggressive. He will keep arguing his point until he convinces his opponent of his views or the opponent tires of the argument and gives in. Ironically, John not only wants to *win* every argument, but he wants his opponent to agree that he (John) is right and to be happy about the outcome. As you can guess, this rarely happens.

- Darlene believes the only way to manage conflict is to *yield* to the other person's point of view, especially if that person is a man. Darlene isn't usually open and honest about the way she feels because she isn't sure the other person will still be her friend if she disagrees openly. Darlene gives in to keep the peace and because she wants to be liked.

- Kyle is a strong supporter of the *compromise* approach to conflict resolution. He is the first person to start making a list of the pros and cons of the different issues in the disagreement. He works with the other person to find a way to incorporate some of both of their ideas in the final outcome. Kyle isn't always happy with the compromises he agrees to, but he feels better when each person "wins" a little, even when it means that each person also "loses" a little.

- Jeff has a different approach to problem solving. He strives to *resolve* the issues. Resolving the issues is different from compromising. Both parties may start out with divergent points of view, but they are willing to work together, pooling ideas, perspectives, perceived possibilities, and energy to find the best solution or make the best decision. A *resolve* approach results in a solution that comes from both persons working together.

By the time they are teens, your children already have developed their own ways to deal with conflict, resolve problems, and make decisions. Their unconscious choices about how to deal with problems usually reflect what they have seen in you.

Running away, pouting, yelling, demanding, always giving in, giving up, or avoiding conflict are nonproductive ways to deal with differences in relationships. Teach your children more productive skills in this area.

As human beings, we are often in conflict with God, but we find that God provides a beautiful role model for us.

- God did not *withdraw* from us. "But God demonstrates his own love for us in this: While we were still sinners, Christ died for us" (Rom. 5:8).

- God did not *win* over us by flaunting holiness and condemning our sinful selves. "For God did not send his Son into the world to condemn the world, but to save the world through him" (John 3:17).

- God does not *yield* to our sinful rebellion against righteousness. "Whoever does not believe stands condemned already because he has not believed in the name of God's one and only Son" (John 3:18).

- God does not *compromise* with us. "Jesus answered, 'I am the way and the truth and the life. No one comes to the Father except through me'" (John 14:6).

- Instead, God *guides* us through our problems and *forgives* our failures through the atoning work of His Son. " 'Come now, let us reason together,' says the LORD. 'Though your sins are like scarlet, they shall be as white as snow; though they are red as crimson, they shall be like wool' " (Is. 1:18).

Children learn to love from watching you

Your children learn how to express their love and affection for others by watching you. What have you been teaching them?

- Sharon expresses love by giving gifts. She sends cards and flowers, makes craft items to give away, and sometimes spends money she doesn't have to give a special gift to a friend. She never goes to a friend's house without a token of affection. While giving presents is a wonderful way to express love and affection, it appears that Sharon is attempting to buy or ensure love with her gift. Sharon's children have learned to share their toys and give freely to others. However, they may grow up believing that to have people like you, you have to give them gifts.

- Trisha expresses love by doing things for others. She runs errands, baby-sits, sews, cooks, and even comes over and cleans her friends' houses. She is a wonderful "servant"-type friend. You can ask Trisha to do anything, and she will respond delightedly. Unfortunately, in her zeal to show love and affection to her friends, she often neglects her family. Once her daughter asked why she was always cooking for her friends but served sandwiches at home because she was "too tired to cook." It is important to teach children that love should be demonstrated by our actions, not only through words. However, Trisha does not seem to have an appropriate balance between showing love and affection for others and showing it to her family. She may be teaching her children that you have to serve others to earn their love and affection.

- Larry expresses love and affection in physical ways. He rarely passes one of his children without giving a quick hug, a ruffle of the hair, a pat on the shoulder, a big smile, or without touching the child in some way. He is not bashful about letting other people see that he is fond of his kids. He also expresses love in physical actions toward his wife. Kissing, hugging, holding hands, and putting his arm around her shoulders are common behaviors. Larry, however, rarely says "I love you." He is not comfortable verbalizing his feelings. Larry is teaching his children the importance of expressing physical affection, but he may also be teaching them that it is not necessary to talk about love.

- Patsy, on the other hand, is extremely comfortable and adept at expressing love and affection in well-chosen words. Sometimes she even embarrasses her children with her lavish praise. The great thing Patsy's children have learned is that "I love you" is nice to hear and easy to say.

What are your children learning about expressing love and affection? Do they see a balanced picture of parents who love and care for one another in many ways—by listening, sharing, doing, giving, serving, touching, and paying attention? This is a goal you will want to achieve.

Look at the ways God demonstrates His love for us. Jesus was a gift (John 3:16–17), as is faith (Eph. 2:8–9), and we know that all good gifts come from God (James 1:17). God talks with us (Is. 1:18), listens to us (Matt. 6:8–15), protects us (John 10:11–16), desires to spend time with us (Matt. 28:20; John 15:4–10), provides for us (Matt. 6:25–34), forgives us (1 John 1:9), and answers our prayers (John 16:23–24). Teach your kids the full kaleidoscope of love's expressions.

It may be a bit frightening and disconcerting to think that you are always on display, being watched and copied by your children. But that is the reality of life and one of the aspects of parenting you must accept. Take a look at what you are teaching your children by your example. Is the message you are sending the one you want your children to receive? Unfortunately, a parent who sets a good example is not guaranteed model children, as Eli and David in the Bible found out. You are not responsible for your children's decisions, only for setting a good example.

By Your Manners

Even at 70 years of age and after being married for 50 years, Stan still says please and thank-you to his wife, Nancy. Stan still opens doors for Nancy, helps her off with her coat, takes her arm when crossing the street, and never interrupts when she is talking. Nancy also treats Stan with perfect courtesy. Because of this, people sometimes remark that Nancy and Stan act more like friends than a married couple.

When your relationship communicates that you and your spouse value one another, care about one another, and believe that what the other is saying is worth listening to, you can teach your children good things.

Mutual support is part of what the apostle Paul is referring to when he talks about being submissive (Ephesians 5). There is a difference between merely expressing love and affection and treating one another with courtesy and respect. If you want your children to learn to treat their spouses with courtesy and respect, set the example now!

By Your Mouth

Following her divorce four years ago, Alice became a single mother with three teenagers. Because of her former husband's behavior, Alice is distrustful of all men. She has often made extremely negative comments, such as "You can't trust men;" "They never do what they say they will;" "Men only want one thing from women;" "They are basically selfish and childish;" "They want their own way all the time and don't care about women."

Is it any wonder that her teenage daughters have failed to develop positive relationships with boys? What have your children learned about relating to the opposite sex by listening to you? Choose your words carefully.

Let your children know what you expect of them

You are responsible for teaching your children scriptural standards for personal conduct. Teach them that God's rules are designed to protect and preserve us (Deut. 6:7–20; Eph. 6:4). Make your own rules and expectations for behavior clear. Helping children grow up to understand the complexities of relationships means more than just throwing out pat phrases such as:

"Be nice."

"Treat people the way you would want to be treated."

"Stick to your principles."

"Learn to listen to what the other person is saying."

These are nice things to say, but children learn more from interaction and discussion than from hearing you repeat such phrases. Talk through what it means to be nice, especially when it is hard to do. Discuss ways to ensure that one's behavior is acceptable and not offensive, even under difficult circumstances. Discuss how it feels when someone treats you nicely or values and respects your opinions. Also talk about how it feels to be mistreated. Invite your children to share their feelings and ideas. As they interact with the subject, they will be learning at a deeper level than if they just memorized a bunch of maxims. And you will be gaining valuable insights into your child's values and thought processes.

Share God's ideals with your kids

The Bible is full of principles that cover our relationships with others. God has high expectations of us in this area. Spend time discussing what the Bible says about how we are to treat people and what these guidelines mean for our relationships. Read Scripture verses in various translations to get the full meaning of what is written.

Discuss how God's standards for our relationships are not just ways to control us and take our fun away. These standards are for our own good and help protect us.

Some helpful passages include: Eph. 4:22–32; Phil. 2:3–5; Col. 3:1–17; 1 Thess. 4:1–9; 1 Thess. 5:14–23; and 2 Peter 1:3–8.

Watch your words

We all say things we don't mean, and we don't expect other adults to take us literally all the time. But be aware of who else is listening. Your children may take what you say at face value and at some level, adopt it as a belief. When Alice says that men can't be trusted, she might be referring to the child support check she hasn't received despite her former husband's promise to be on time. Her daughter, hearing the comment, may begin to believe that all men can't be trusted—ever.

We are cautioned to put aside idle talk and not to engage in meaningless conversations (1 Tim. 6:20; 2 Tim. 2:16; James 1:26). Be very careful about the actual words that come out of your mouth. Not only might your children be listening, but Jesus said we will be held accountable for our spoken words (Matt. 12:36).

Tom freely expresses his appreciation of beautiful women. Some of his comments are appropriate; others may give his son the wrong impression. When Tom sees a well-known sports figure with a less-than-stunning woman, he sometimes makes derogatory comments such as "What's he doing with that dog?" When talking about the type of girl he would like to date, Tom's son has often said she must be a beautiful, perfect-sized person.

Tom is inadvertently teaching his son that looks are the most important feature in a date. Tom would be much wiser to teach his son that there is a significant difference between the outward appearance and the inner person (1 Sam. 16:7).

What's the Answer?

Like it or not, you are God's audiovisual aid for teaching your children about relationships. If you are the perfect example, have perfect manners, and always say the right things, you are truly unusual. Most of us, from time to time, find ourselves embarrassed by what we might have said or done in a certain situation. We hope our children learn to do what is right and not copy what was said or done in a moment of weakness.

As a Christian parent, you have the power of the Holy Spirit to draw upon in your life. Through the Spirit's power, you can learn to become a better example for your children. Always be ready to learn better ways to communicate what your children need to hear. Change your behaviors so your kids see the correct ways to do things. Transferring your values to your children is an exciting challenge. Seeing them choose God's ideals as their standards for conduct is the most rewarding time in your life. It makes every past moment of worry and struggle worth it.

2

WHAT IS A
DATE?

*Candy called her friend Donna to see if her teenage
daughter, Sandra, could baby-sit for an hour while she
went to get her hair cut.*

"Sorry," Donna said. "Sandra has a date."

*"You let your 13-year-old daughter date?" Candy
asked incredulously. "I can't believe that. I've told my
daughter she can't date until she's 16."*

*"I don't see anything wrong with letting Sandra go
bowling with a boy from her class on a Saturday afternoon," Donna responded. "A group of eight kids is going
together. One of the parents is driving, and they'll only be
gone for a couple of hours."*

*"Oh," Candy answered. "That's different. Bowling in
a group isn't a date. I thought you meant you let her go out
on a **real** date."*

One of the first issues in addressing kids' dating
is defining the term *date*. That's not as easy as it
sounds. One group of parents tried.

*"It's a **date** when you go somewhere or do something
you would not do with a same-sex friend," Bob said. Then*

he realized that was really a poor definition because one can go out to dinner with a friend of either sex.

"It's a **date** when who you are with is more important than what you do or where you go," Tom suggested. But that definition might fit situations that clearly are not dates, such as going out with a friend, a relative, or an important person from your community.

"It's a **date** whenever you go out alone with a member of the opposite sex," Mary said. Then she contradicted herself, "But if I meet a business associate for lunch, who happens to be a man, that's not a date. But how would I explain double dates or group dates?"

Lynn laughed. "Sounds like we don't know how to explain what a **date** is. It seems to me that all we've done so far is agree that a date may be (or may not be) any time you get together with a member of the opposite sex."

"Maybe a **date** involves an emotional expectation— some kind of romantic significance in being together. There's a desire to pursue the development of the relationship," Marvin said thoughtfully.

What is a *date*? Who knows? A date is what you define it to be. It is not important that you come up with the ultimate and perfect definition of what a date *is*. Rather, you need to define what activities you will permit your children to participate in with the opposite sex, at what age, and whether they can be alone, with other kids, or in a chaperoned situation. That is a tall order.

Consider these situations.

Casual Meetings

In our parents' day, kids often met after school or on Saturday afternoons at the drugstore. In later years, they met at the malt shop, the A & W Drive-In, or the coffee shop. Today, kids might meet in any number of places—a pizza parlor, a fast-food restaurant, a video arcade, or at a friend's house. What is acceptable to you for your kids to do?

- Can they meet other kids if there is a group involved? What if there are other kids, but all of them are paired off? Is it okay if they go alone and someone shows up and joins them? Is it okay if the meeting isn't planned?

- Can they stop somewhere on the way home from school if they want to or are invited to do so? Must your children get prior permission from you each time?

- Can they go get a hamburger alone with a *friend* of the opposite sex (such as the boy next door) if there is no suggestion of a romantic involvement? What if they have been doing this for several months and a romance flares up? Should they stop going to get something to eat together?

Formal Events

The youth group at church hosts a Sweethearts'

Dinner on February 14th. You don't allow your son to date yet, but the group expectation is that participants will come as couples. Will you make an exception for this event and allow your son to ask a girl to go with him?

Proms, banquets, and other formal events are often planned for couples. Perhaps this ought to be changed, but for now, that's the way it is. In some cases, attendance together is one way to publicly declare an ongoing relationship between two teenagers. In other cases, asking someone to attend with you is nothing more than a way of being accepted by the rest of the group because you didn't attend alone.

Formal events usually involve a lot of other people. There may be less danger of inappropriate behavior occurring between the dating "couple." The only time they may be alone is the drive to and from the event. This may be a consideration when deciding whether to allow your son or daughter to go. If the "drive time" is a concern, consider providing the transportation.

Group Events

"Even though my daughter has started dating, I still have some guidelines she must follow until she's older," Rose admits. *"She can only go on 'dates' to group events, and the more active the better. Bowling, sports events,*

chaperoned parties, youth group activities, swimming, bik-ing, in-line skating, and volleyball are my choices for her. So far, she's been agreeable."

Group events are a good way for your kids to begin experiencing the dynamics of dating. If they are under 16, they usually must walk or be driven by you or an older sibling. During the event, there is usually involvement with other participants, and the "couple" is often not totally alone or absorbed in one another. Rose is wise to suggest active events. It is much healthier for kids to actively participate in events than to spend long hours sitting on the couch with dimmed lights, listening to music, and focusing on each other.

Double Dating

At some point, your kids will want to limit the number of other people who are a part of their date. Perhaps an interim step between group events and dating alone is double dating. However, depending on who the other couple is, this may or may not deter wrong choices. A couple necking and petting in the front seat of the car is not going to stop most kids from necking and petting in the back seat.

But double dating can be helpful, particularly if the other couple is older and committed to encourag-ing the younger couple to have fun, keep the date healthy, and make proper choices.

Dating Alone

"I feel as if my son has hit a major milestone tonight," Owen confessed to his neighbor. *"He and his girlfriend went on their first 'alone' date."*

Finally there comes the day when your kids are allowed to date by themselves. That's when the rules for dating (see chapter 6) are tested, and you may begin to lose some sleep. Many parents limit the dates at first until they are convinced the kids will abide by the rules and behave responsibly. Afternoon events, established time limits, and planned activities (preferably with others around such as at a ball game) often provide the ground rules for the first solo dates kids experience.

Later, you may allow your kids to dine out, go to the movies, and participate in more intimate dates. Of course, your kids will probably believe they are ready for the latter long before you think they are.

Going Steady

"My son announced at dinner last night that he and Amy are 'going steady,' " Karen shared with Jill. "I didn't know what to say. He's only 11! He doesn't 'date.' When I asked what going steady meant, he said that it meant he liked Amy and that she liked him. Going steady meant that everyone knew that they liked each other and not anyone else in the same way."

To kids, *going steady* means different things at different developmental stages. Implicit in the term at any age is a commitment (in some form) to have a special relationship with one person and to exclude others from similar relationships. However, the commitment is often short-lived and easily broken at younger ages. Most parents don't get too concerned about preteens saying they are *going steady* as long as the term does not signify a physical relationship involving kissing, prolonged hugging, or more intimate touching.

A valid concern with exclusivity in younger relationships is the lost opportunities to relate with different people and learn from each of those relationships. Children who don't have a variety of relationships are likely to miss out on learning to appreciate different personality types, learning to adjust to different problem-solving techniques, and determining which types of persons they enjoy spending time with. They won't experience different conversational styles or determine what makes it easier to share things with one person. Experiencing different people in a dating relationship is a critical developmental need.

Older teens often use the term *going steady* as a precursor to a more serious relationship, such as an engagement. *Going steady* is not binding or intended to last forever. It is not unusual, however, for one of the parties to have stronger expectations for a permanent future than the other. When the relationship breaks off, there can be a lot of pain.

Engaged

After dating someone for a while and perhaps *going steady* for a period of time, a couple may get engaged. This commitment is intended to further prepare them for marriage. It is a time to get to know each other better, learning how to relate to one another and develop skills for a successful married life. The engagement is also necessary to prepare for the wedding, which usually requires a great deal of planning and a lot of money.

An engagement that takes place soon after the first date is something you will probably want to discourage. If either party in the engagement has little or no dating experience, the engagement could be a problem. The couple hasn't had time to fully realize some of the ways men and women are different in our culture and to learn to relate to those differences in successful ways.

Discuss and Agree on Definitions

Lance and his parents had several conversations about dating. They discussed what constituted a date and what types of dates were and were not allowed at his age. Lance knew just where his parents stood, and they were sure that he understood their expectations.

To hold your teenagers accountable, you need to be clear in your own mind what level of interaction with the opposite sex you will allow at what age. While your teenagers will probably disagree with your limitations, it is your prerogative to set the limits for your kids. However, don't make the mistake of making the decision without talking with your spouse and with your kids. Times have changed since you were dating, and definitions may also have changed. Talk about these issues long before your kids are old enough to date and you will save yourself a lot of grief. It is easier to set limitations before a situation arises than to say no when there is a specific event your child wants to attend with a specific individual.

Remember, you won't be able to hold just one conversation on the subject. You will want to revisit the definitions, and the limitations, as your children get older or as other children reach the dating age.

3

HOW WELL DO THEY COMMUNICATE?

"I'm fairly comfortable with the idea that Ellen will be dating soon," Doug confided to his friend, Mark. "She's self-assured, very assertive, and speaks up for herself. She has strong opinions and a commitment to living by her convictions. I don't think she would be easily convinced by her friends, or a date, to do something she doesn't believe is right. Also she's been very responsible about coming home on time or letting us know if she's going to be late."

"I'm not surprised," Mark responded. "I've always admired the way you've trained your kids to speak up. They are respectful but not shy about disagreeing with anyone."

One of your parental functions is to train your kids in effective communication. That training shouldn't start when they become teenagers. It should start whenever they attempt to express themselves, even at a very young age. You need to cultivate your children's ability to communicate from the beginning. While it can be tempting to tell a talkative 5-year-old to be quiet, to go out and play, or that she doesn't know what she is talking about, be careful not to shut her down. Although you don't have to allow your children to join in every conversation, make time to listen to them, encourage them to express their ideas and opinions, and discuss things together, no matter how childish or uninformed their opinions may be.

Listening to your children shows them they are valued and that you respect their opinions, even if you don't agree with them. If your children are not allowed to verbalize their ideas, they may grow up believing acceptance is based on going along with what others are saying and not expressing dissenting opinions. This can be a problem when the crowd is trying to convince your teenager to go somewhere he or she is not allowed to go or do something he or she knows is wrong.

A second communication skill you need to help your children develop is how to ask for what they want (not demand). They shouldn't expect people to be mind readers and automatically rescue them or take care of them. Teenagers who have not learned to ask for what they want or who have poor self-esteem often find themselves going along with the crowd or yielding to their dates' desires.

A third communication skill your teenagers

need, and one that can be learned early on, is how to refuse unreasonable or unacceptable requests. Do not confuse this with disobedience (refusing to obey those in authority because the child believes the rule to be unreasonable). Rather, it is the ability to stand firm in one's convictions, avoid being used or abused, and to insist on being treated with respect by one's friends and dates. It also includes setting necessary limits on how far to go and when to tell someone to stop.

These three skills are very important for young children. They become even more essential as your kids grow into mature relationships. These skills are best learned early in life, but it is never too late to learn. And the best classroom is the home.

Teaching Kids to Speak Up

Shirley is not comfortable expressing her opinions or ideas. She usually waits until she has heard what others have to say and then agrees with the majority opinion. Rick, on the other hand, is very vocal. He has an opinion about everything and is not shy about speaking up. He expects everyone to accept what he has to say and go along with him.

In between these two extremes, you will find more productive approaches to being honest with others about what you think or believe. Encourage your children to listen respectfully and with an open mind to the ideas of others. Then they should form their own opinions and be willing to voice and even defend them. Peter talks about knowing what we believe and being ready to explain it in appropriate circumstances (1 Peter 3:15).

Everyone has ideas and opinions. Some ideas are more informed than others, some are more logical, and some are more creative. Some ideas will work and others will not. Some will prove accurate and appropriate and others will not. When shared and discussed, ideas and opinions tend to get sorted out, clarified, and become more useful. Remember how Andrew brought the little boy with his five loaves and two fishes to Jesus? Andrew had part of an idea and Jesus had the rest. Together, through the miraculous power of the Lord Jesus, the five thousand were fed (John 6:1–13).

Understand the reasons people don't speak up

- They don't want to be considered foolish.

The real reason Shirley doesn't speak up is that she doesn't want to appear foolish. She hasn't read all the latest information on a subject, and she doesn't have a good memory for details. Because of these things, her friends have teased her about her ideas in the past. Shirley doesn't want to risk additional rejection, so she has become a quiet person.

Until she becomes comfortable speaking up,

Shirley needs to practice doing so in nonthreatening situations. She can pick the time to take such risks and the subjects about which she is willing to speak. With time and practice, Shirley can become less afraid of appearing foolish.

- They don't want to show how little they know.

Roger has always been the studious type and has little interest in sports. He isn't comfortable participating in conversations about sports because he doesn't know the rules of football, basketball, or soccer or the names (or records) of the major figures of each game. When Roger can't avoid being in situations where sports are the topic of conversation, he withdraws from the conversation.

Roger needs to learn either to gather some basic information on topics about which he feels uninformed or to accept the fact that he is not well-versed in every subject. Then he can learn to ask interesting and conversation-generating questions. This would involve Roger in the conversation and keep it going as others do most of the talking.

- They don't want to argue.

Mona is seriously afraid of disagreements and arguments. Because she is convinced that someone in the group will always disagree with her, she rarely shares what she is thinking or feeling. People see Mona as easy to get along with, and they expect her to go along with the crowd, which she does, even when she has deep reservations.

A fear of conflict can be a major reason people fail to speak up. Learning conflict resolution skills will be discussed in the next chapter of this book.

- They do not want to accept responsibility.

Ken was with a group of his friends who wanted to go to a teenage music club. Because Ken suspected that kids would be using drugs at the club, he argued with his friends that they could listen to music some place else and have as much fun without risking getting into trouble. His friends reluctantly agreed not to go to the club, but they insisted that Ken make the arrangements for the alternative activity. Ken wasn't sure where to start!

Often when we speak up, criticize someone else's ideas, or voice our opinion, we end up getting pressured into accepting responsibility to implement our ideas and change the group's mind. That's a heavy responsibility, one some teenagers do not want to accept.

- They don't want to be proven wrong.

James almost never speaks up because he hates to be wrong. When he ventures an idea and someone explains why it won't work, James becomes embarrassed and angry that his idea was not the best. Over the years, James has chosen to keep quiet rather than risk being proven wrong. This habit could be a problem when he begins dating and even more of one when he enters the work force or gets married.

Most of us have experienced similar fears about expressing our ideas. No one wants to get into an argument, be rejected, proven wrong, or ridiculed. Learning how to express ourselves and our ideas without antagonizing others can be an invaluable asset in interpersonal communications. Help your children develop this skill.

Prepare your children to speak up

As you help your children learn to speak up, remember these truths.

- God has not called us to a lifestyle of fear.

According to 2 Tim. 1:7, we are not to live in the bondage of fear. There is a promise that through the power of the Holy Spirit, we will be able to speak our minds and express our faith openly. Others do not have to agree with our ideas for them to be valuable and valid. Our lives must follow God's rules of conduct, not what friends or dates expect.

- Your children have access to the power of the Holy Spirit in their thought processes.

In John 14:26, we read that the Holy Spirit will teach us and remind us of things we have been taught. If we, and our children, pray for guidance, God will hear us and send His Spirit to help (James 1:5).

- Your children don't have to be like everyone else. No one person is a clone of another. We are all unique individuals, designed and created by God. We are God's workmanship (Eph. 2:10). Your children are not carbon copies of their friends. Instill in your children an appreciation for the differences in people.

- The goal is not to force others to agree with you.

While it is important that your children learn to speak up for themselves, it is equally important that they understand their opinions and ideas cannot be forced upon others. There will be disagreements and points of difference—even between friends.

- Focus on expressing yourself clearly rather than on how other people may respond.

Remember Peter at Pentecost (Acts 2:14–39)? He had an unpopular message to deliver as he told the crowd how the Son of God had been crucified and rejected. But Peter spoke boldly, articulately, and concisely. Teach your children to express themselves clearly and boldly, to respect the differences of others, and not to worry about the response. Of course, considering the possible responses is one way to decide what to say and how to say it.

- The mental picture you project will determine how afraid you are.

Dorothy wanted to invite a group of friends to her house for a party. Every time she thought of doing so, she saw herself asking them and heard them making silly excuses and refusing to come. She pictured herself feeling rejected and embarrassed.

When her mother asked why she had not invited her friends over, Dorothy shared her fears. Dorothy's mother asked her to change her mental picture of the event. "Picture yourself asking them to come to a fun party. Then picture them eagerly accepting. How would you feel then?" she asked Dorothy.

"I'd be happy," Dorothy admitted. She decided to change her mental picture and practiced her invitation over and over in her mind. When she did invite her friends, it was with the confidence that they would eagerly accept, which, of course, they did.

Help your children practice speaking up

Here are some suggestions to help your children practice speaking up and expressing their ideas and opinions.

- Bring up a controversial topic, perhaps from the local newspaper, and ask each family member to give their opinions or ideas. Don't belittle any opinion. Weigh what is said and consider the merits of each idea. Allow healthy, positive interaction among family members. There can be questions and even a little debate, but each opinion must be accepted as a worthwhile point of view. If you insist that siblings shouldn't make fun of each other's opinions, this indicates that you value the input of each family member.

- When you talk with your children, ask them to express their opinions. Listen attentively and interact positively with the ideas they express.

- When there is a problem, include your children in the brainstorming process for possible solutions.

- Quote a particularly valuable opinion expressed by one of your children to the family and give him or her credit for the idea.

- Even though you must insist on obedience with house rules, allow your children to express their feelings and ideas about the rules or the consequences.

- Watch family-oriented situation comedies on television. Be on the alert for instances when someone expresses an opinion. After the show, discuss what happened. Was the opinion accepted, rejected, ridiculed, or acted upon? Ask your children what they think the character felt about the response his or her idea received. Ask if they have ever been in a similar situation and how they felt. Ask if there was a better way for the character to express the idea or if there was a better way to respond.

Teaching Kids to Ask for What They Want

When Howard was four, his mother told him not to greet his grandfather each time he visited with "Did you bring me a present?" She told him it wasn't nice to ask for presents.

When Howard was 10, his father took him to antique car shows (which was his father's hobby). Each time, his father told him, "Don't embarrass me by asking stupid questions. Just be quiet and listen, and you will learn." Howard tried, but usually his questions weren't answered unless he asked them.

When Howard was 11, his parents rented a car for two days while theirs was being repaired. Howard's dad could have ridden to work with a neighbor, and Howard volunteered to find his own rides to school. But his parents didn't want to ask for favors. They said it was important to be independent and not to burden friends with requests for help.

When Howard was 12, the family took a cross-country trip. The most memorable part for Howard was the number of times they got lost. His father simply refused to stop and ask for directions. "Don't like to bother people. I'll figure it out," his father would insist.

When Howard was 13, his mother strained her back lifting heavy boxes while cleaning the garage. When Howard asked why she hadn't waited for his father to come home from work or for him to come home from school, his mother admitted that she hated asking for help. "I feel like I'm saying I'm weak or that I can't do something if I have to ask for help," she said.

Is it any wonder that Howard is not skilled at

asking for what he wants? Asking does not mean that you will always receive. People still have the option of refusing your requests. But not asking means you expect others to read your mind and know what you are thinking, wanting, or needing, which is unreasonable. Not asking also means you may have to handle the situation yourself. Learning to ask appropriately for what you want is an important skill, especially for young people who are beginning to develop dating relationships and, eventually, committed relationships.

Be clear about what requests you believe to be appropriate

Marge has no problem asking for anything and everything. If she likes what you serve for dinner, she will ask for a portion to take home. If she likes your earrings, she may ask if you would give them to her. She asks to borrow money, clothes, cars, and anything else she wants. She asks inappropriately at times.

Keith, on the other hand, doesn't ask for enough. He will die of thirst before asking for a glass of water. He will walk four miles rather than ask for a ride. He just won't ask for anything.

As a parent, think through what you want to teach your children to request.

- It's okay to ask for information.

When Jesus talked to the woman at the well, she

quickly asked for information, for answers to questions that puzzled her (John 4:7–13).

Teach your children to take the initiative to obtain information, especially if it is easily accessible from a book or a phone call. If the information is only available from a person, encourage them to become comfortable asking for the information they need. This includes directions, repeated explanations from a teacher, or clarification about party details from friends (who will be there, what activities will be involved, and will there be any drinking or drugs).

- It's okay to ask for favors sometimes.

Good friends don't mind, and sometimes enjoy, doing favors for one another. If you truly need or want company, it is acceptable to occasionally ask a friend to go out of his or her way to do something for you.

However, always asking for favors can be a sign of insecurity. It may indicate that your child only feels loved when someone is doing something for him or her. On the other hand, never asking for favors may be a sign of low self-esteem. This could indicate your child is afraid no one likes him or her enough to want to help.

Your kids need to know how to ask for favors in case they need help. Getting another ride home from a party when his or her partner has been drinking or doing drugs is one situation in which this skill could be critical.

When teaching your kids to ask for favors, remember that they need to be:

1. Willing to do the same for a friend when asked.

2. Gracious if the request is denied.

3. Independent, resourceful, and able to take care of themselves when help from friends is not available.

There are lots of role models in the Bible who asked for what they wanted: Elijah asked the widow of Zarephath to feed him (1 Kings 17:8–16); Jarius asked Jesus to heal his daughter (Mark 5:22–42); and Paul asked Philemon to take back Onesimus for his sake (Philemon 1–21).

- It's okay to ask for help.

Peter didn't hesitate to call for help when he started sinking in the water (Matt. 14:28–31). Train your children to seek help in times of emergency (running out of gas, when they need to separate from a person or group because of inappropriate behavior, etc.).

In life, however, we sometimes need help with more mundane things. Some jobs require more than one person to be successfully completed. When that is true, it is perfectly acceptable to ask for assistance. In fact, not to do so would be foolish. Besides, working together on something helps build healthier relationships as partners.

- It's okay to ask for emotional support.

Being a teenager is possibly one of the most diffi-cult roles your kids will face. Kids who stand up for what they believe may be ridiculed, belittled, and rejected. Kids are pressured by their dates, their peers, and their friends to become sexually involved. Kids who adhere to God's principles often believe they are in the minority. They feel like Elijah did when he thought he was the only person in all of Israel who was remaining true to God (1 Kings 19:14). Kids may get depressed, angry, and upset at times and need emotional support.

Your kids need to learn that it is acceptable to share what is happening in their lives and to ask for emotional support when needed. Your teenagers may not want to give you all the details, but if you're sen-sitive, you can acknowledge that something is wrong and invite your teens to share as much as possible.

Your kids need to be able to come home and admit that it's been a bad day and conversation at dinner is not something in which they want to partic-ipate. That doesn't necessarily mean they ought to sulk, refuse to help with the dishes, or get out of other chores. It does mean they are entitled to some extra emotional support.

- It's okay to ask for attention.

Teach your children to ask for your time and atten-tion when they feel they need it. This may be to discuss an issue, work on a project, get help with homework, or play a game. As a parent, you sometimes miss the subtle and not-so-subtle clues that indicate your children need attention. Teach them to ask.

Understand why people don't ask for what they want

When asked why they don't feel comfortable asking others for what they want, people give different reasons/excuses.

- *"Asking is imposing on friends."*
- *"Asking makes me vulnerable. If I ask, someone knows what to do to hurt me; that is, they can refuse my request."*
- *"Others don't want to help me."*
- *"If I ask others to do something for me, they will expect me to do something for them."*
- *"I expect people to be aware of me and what I need so that I don't have to ask."*

These reasons or excuses usually are a result of poor self-esteem and a lack of understanding that it really is acceptable to ask for what you want. Help your children get past these misconceptions.

Prepare your children to learn to ask for what they want

Consider these guidelines when working with your children.

- Requests need to be reasonable.

Most of us think our expectations of others are reasonable, at least at first. Sometimes when we think them through, we find that our expectations are not reasonable. Expecting your best friend not to have other friends is unreasonable. Asking someone to cancel prior plans and come over to do what you want to do may be unreasonable. Insisting that someone do something "right this minute" (because that's when you need the help) may be unreasonable.

Reasonable requests take into consideration the other person's needs. They do not ask for sacrifices or make unreasonable demands on the individual's time. Perhaps most importantly, reasonable requests can be accomplished by the person being asked.

- Requests need to be clear.

Sally always thinks she is being clear about what she is asking, but she is often very vague. Sally called a friend and asked if she would come over that afternoon. The friend agreed and arrived at 4:30 p.m., stayed for an hour, and went home. Sally was upset.

Sally had wanted her friend to come over at 1 p.m. and stay through supper. But Sally didn't make her request clear. Misunderstandings in relationships often develop because one of the persons isn't skilled in making clear requests. Sally needs to work on being more specific in her requests.

- Requests are not demands.

Although it has been said before, it is important that your kids learn early that requests are *requests* and not *demands*. People must be given permission to refuse requests without feeling guilty.

- Timing is important.

Often the most important aspect of asking for what you want is the timing of your request. When people are tired, busy, frustrated, or angry, they will probably not be as receptive to a request for information, a favor, help, or attention. Help your children learn to consider the situation of the other person before jumping immediately into a request mode.

Help your children practice asking for what they want

Here are some suggestions to help your children practice asking for what they want.

- When your children make a nonspecific request, ask them to rephrase it until you have the information you need (what, when, where, how much, what kind, etc.).

- Make a game out of asking. Write 20 to 30 situations on slips of paper and put them in a bowl. Each family member draws one out and must phrase the request indicated by the situation.

- Invite your kids to share requests they receive at

school and explain whether the requests were specific, clear, and reasonable.

- Write a list of nonspecific requests and give them to your kids. Give them 10 minutes to rewrite them into clear, specific, and reasonable requests.

- Be sure your own requests are appropriate, clear, and specific.

Teaching Kids to Refuse Unreasonable Requests

Irene says no easily and often. Too often. Eric finds it impossible to refuse any request, however unreasonable. Both have problems.

It is important that you teach your children to say no when appropriate. If they can't develop this skill, your kids will find others are dictating their choices, using up their free time, keeping them from doing what they want or what is right, or using them.

Understand why limits are important

- Without limits, your child's time will be spread too thin.

Eric helps his friends with homework, yard work, and chores. He is so involved at school (even in some activities that don't interest him personally) that he doesn't get home until just before dinner. He is active at church and puts in extra time on the weekends working with the younger chil-

dren's activities. Because he wants to make good grades, Eric studies late every night. He is tired, overcommitted, and needs to learn to set limits in his life.

- Without limits, the requests keep coming in.

Until Eric learns to say no, people will continue to ask him to participate, help, and do things. The word is out that "Eric will do it." Ironically, even those people who are aware that they are imposing will continue to ask. They will bring the next request with a comment such as, "I know I've already asked a lot, but would you ..."

- Without limits, your child won't have a personal life.

The other day, Eric's mother asked him what he was going to do that weekend for fun. "Fun?" he answered. "I don't have time for fun. I'm too busy." Too busy is right, even a 17-year-old needs time for himself.

- Without limits, your child may begin to be untruthful.

The other night, Eric received a phone call asking him to do something the next night. Not knowing how to say no, Eric lied. He said he was sorry and that he would say yes if he could, but he was committed to help someone else. That was not true. Eric needed to study for an exam, but he didn't feel comfortable saying no to someone, even when he needed to do something for himself.

Recognize why it may be hard for your child to say no

Eric's mother recognized the problem and sat down with Eric one evening. Because Eric agreed that he had a problem that was adversely affecting his life, she asked him to share the reasons he felt he could not say no comfortably. Eric had several.

- If it was a good cause, Eric felt he couldn't say no.
In the last year, Eric has helped with special olympics, the March of Dimes fundraiser, the junior class work day, the youth group car wash, packaging food for the homeless, collecting signatures for an election issue, the school play, the church cantata, and he has stuffed envelopes for a political candidate.

"How do you say you don't want to help if you think the cause is a good one?" Eric asked.

Eric needs to learn to budget his time and give a certain amount to good causes, school, church, and leisure activities and say no to all other requests.

- If someone helped him out, Eric felt he could never say no to that person.
What Eric needs to understand is that reciprocity is appropriate, but one favor does not get repaid one hundred fold. There is no obligation to pay back and keep paying back favors from friends.

- If the request came from a friend, Eric felt he could not say no because friends don't refuse friends.

When Eric's mom asked if any of his friends ever said no to him, he admitted they did. Frequently, as a matter of fact. She asked if Eric liked his friends less because of their refusal of his requests. "No," Eric said thoughtfully. "I just assume they have something else to do."

"Then why isn't it okay for you to have other plans sometimes?" his mother asked gently.

- If he said no, Eric felt badly about himself.

Probably the hardest person on Eric is Eric. When he doesn't live up to his expectation that friends never say no or that one doesn't say no to good causes, he feels guilty and vows never to say no again.

Eric has some serious retraining to do to see things differently and learn to say no when appropriate.

Prepare your children to refuse unreasonable requests

As you help your children learn to refuse unreasonable requests, remember these truths.

- Discover which types of requests are a problem.

Do your children have difficulty refusing to lend money or clothes, to help with homework, to go somewhere they don't want to, to protect a friend who is lying, to go along with the crowd, to allow a fellow student to cheat, to do drugs, to cover up rule infractions, or to become physically or sexually involved with a member of the opposite sex?

Discovering where the problems lie is the important first step. Some children have trouble refusing any requests; others have problems refusing certain types of requests. Perhaps the issue is not with the request but with the person doing the asking. Do your children have problems refusing inappropriate requests from bosses, teachers, friends, dates, or persons in authority?

When the lame man asked Peter and John for alms, Peter had to refuse that request because it was unreasonable, given their financial circumstances. Peter and John didn't have any money to give the man (Acts 3:2–8).

When Martha asked Jesus to make her sister Mary come help with the chores, Jesus refused. He said that what Mary was doing was better than chores (Luke 10:38–42).

• Develop strategies for saying no kindly but firmly.

The refusal doesn't need to be angry, aggressive, or an attack, but it does need to be firm. Help your children learn to cushion their refusals in acceptable phrases such as "I can't do that this time;" "That's just not my style (preference/choice/belief/plan);" or "I have other plans that night, so I won't be able to go."

When it comes to some situations, the refusal needs to be quite direct—"Do not touch me there" or "I do not do drugs and will not go out with anyone who does." The refusal still needs to be kind and the tone friendly but firm.

- Don't apologize for saying no.

Tell your children not to say they're sorry if they are not actually sorry they can't do something or go somewhere. When learning to refuse unreasonable requests, part of the lesson is to take responsibility for your stance.

There were times in Jesus' life when He said no to the needs and requests of others. The multitudes sometimes followed Him for long days. He would heal them, teach them, and finally say enough and send them away (Matt. 14:13–22).

- Don't lie about why you are saying no.

Although it is not required, people are often tempted to soften their refusal by giving an explanation. Occasionally, an explanation sounds good and cushions the refusal, but it is untruthful. Remind your children that we are expected to tell the truth at all times. If they give an explanation, it needs to be truthful.

- Be prepared for a negative response.

The responses to your children's refusals may range from a shrug of the shoulders and an "oh, well" to outright anger. At first, your children will be tempted to retract their no and do what is being asked. They must learn to get past this temptation and stand firm in their faith and convictions.

Help your children practice refusing unreasonable requests

Here are some suggestions to help your children practice refusing unreasonable requests.

- Spend time role-playing. Have one family member ask another to do something (give a back rub, exchange chores, help with a project, share a treasured possession, go on an errand, etc.). The person who is asked should practice saying no in a kind, firm, and appropriate way. After each role-play, family members should critique one another and help work on the refusing skills.

- Tell stories about problems that have resulted from not being able to say no. As parents, you probably have stories of your own that will help your children see the problems caused when someone gives in to unreasonable requests. Encourage your children to tell their own stories.

- Read the story of Daniel and his friends when they refused to eat the king's food (Dan. 1:1–21). Discuss the way Daniel and his friends refused the request (order). What was the outcome of the refusal?

- Do a Bible study on stories where people said no. Discuss the techniques they used and the consequences of their refusals. Note that not all the consequences were positive on the human level. However, when someone said no in order to be obedient to God's laws, God honored their decision. (Examples include Joseph refusing Potiphar's wife, David refusing to kill King Saul, Peter and John refusing to stop preaching, and Jesus refusing to stop healing on the Sabbath.)

Why Kids Need to Learn to Communicate Effectively

Communication skills are important for everyone, but so often these skills are honed only after one becomes an adult. One of the best gifts you can give your children is the ability to communicate effectively. This skill will be particularly helpful as they begin to relate to the opposite sex romantically, make a commitment to one person, become engaged, and eventually, get married. Communication skills are just as important for those who do not marry or who wait until later in life to marry. We communicate with others every day, and we need to be skilled in saying what we mean.

In dating relationships, your kids need to be able to express their ideas and opinions so that they do not become people-pleasers. They need to be able to share with their dating partner(s) their convictions, standards, desires, and limits. To do this easily and consistently, your children will need to constantly practice communicating. Speaking up in a romantic relationship can be risky if teens fear that they will lose the relationship as a result.

You want to give your children this message: "You probably will not live with this other person the rest of your life, but you will live with *yourself* the rest of your life. Remember that maintaining your personal integrity is more important than the friendship and acceptance of someone who asks you or pressures you to violate your personal standards. Any person who does pressure you into something you don't want to do does not love you or have your best interests at heart."

It is critical that your kids learn how to ask for what they want. They need to know exactly what they are agreeing to do or where they are agreeing to go. They must be able to set limits on the degree of intimacy they will allow. They need to be able to ask other adults to protect their rights, assist them in escaping from an undesirable situation, or defuse a hostile situation.

Also important is the ability to refuse inappropriate requests. Your children need to be able to tell their dating partner(s) they don't want to go certain places, do drugs, drive or ride in a "borrowed" car, engage in sexual conduct, see an R-rated movie, or be alone together for hours with no adults present. In short, they need to be able to say no to any suggestion or request that makes them feel uncomfortable.

Your job is to do what you can to give your child the skills to communicate.

DO THEY HAVE GOOD RELATIONAL SKILLS?

Randy was a good-looking 16-year-old, an only child, and an only grandchild on both his mother's and father's side. All four grandparents and both parents designed a significant portion of their lives around Randy and his needs and wants. Randy grew up with a slightly distorted view of life and interpersonal relationships. He had a tendency to expect everyone who cared about him to go along with his ideas and desires.

Randy was seriously shocked when Roxanne, his 16-year-old steady girlfriend, disagreed with him on a major issue and refused to give in to his point of view. In the ensuing argument, Randy said some very hurtful words to Roxanne and walked out without resolving anything.

Randy complained to his mother. "Obviously Roxanne doesn't really care about me," he said angrily. "Otherwise she would want to do what I want!"

Randy's mother realized that he had never learned to disagree, argue, or debate, and more importantly, he had never learned to resolve conflicts with the people he loved.

Don't let your children grow up without learning that conflict is an inevitable part of life. Teach them the skills they need to express their points of view, listen to someone else's opinions, work through problems, and resolve them together.

Relationships are difficult because each of us is unique. We think differently, have individual needs, and approach life from different points of view. If your children are to participate in successful intimate relationships, they must become comfortable with differences in others and with their own uniqueness.

Teaching Kids to Accept Differences

Ann was sitting in her family room watching her children. She was struck, not for the first time, by how different each child was. She and Gil had tried to be consistent in their rules, expectations, and discipline, but each child was unique and very different from the others.

Jason was quiet, sensitive, easily hurt, and would do anything to please. Her other son, Jim, was an extrovert who bounced back from almost anything, almost instantly. Failures, disappointments, limitations, problems, disagreements—nothing seemed to phase him for long.

When examining her daughters, Ann saw Gail as serious about her studies, fastidious about her room, careful about her grooming, and intent when doing chores, projects, or homework. She was articulate and outspoken, and her opinions were usually well-thought-out. Suzanne was a warm, playful, cuddly person who seemed to love being with people, working together, helping out, and being involved.

Ann loved each of her children, not only because they were her children but also because of their special qualities. Ann could also see why sibling conflicts and disagreements were common. Jim was impatient with Jason's sensitivity. Gail was intolerant of Suzanne's lack of ambition. Jason believed that Jim had no serious feelings because he never seemed to care enough to be hurt or depressed. Suzanne often felt that Gail was trying to push her and wouldn't accept her for who she was.

But Ann's children had also learned valuable lessons in appreciating differences. When Jason needed to be cheered up, he spent time with Jim, drawing from his ability to bounce back. When Suzanne had an assignment for school, she knew she could count on Gail to help her plan it and suggest ways to complete the project successfully. Gail sometimes took a lesson from Suzanne and abandoned her task-oriented behaviors for an evening of fun. Jim sometimes talked with Jason when he had difficulty understanding a problem with a relationship.

Differences in personalities and approaches to life can cause conflict in any group. Such conflict is most upsetting in intimate relationships where there is a high level of emotional commitment. One can withdraw from a group, but to break off a dating relationship is a more serious decision and may hurt.

It is important for your children to acknowledge and appreciate differences. The challenge of looking at things from a different point of view expands their mental abilities and perspective. Exposure to different people, ideas, activities, and experiences can enhance everyone's life.

Understand why people aren't comfortable with differences

- They aren't sure of themselves.

Individuals with little self-confidence may not be comfortable around those who are different from themselves. They may feel they don't measure up, or they may feel threatened, criticized, or challenged.

- They don't want to have to change.

Some people don't like who they are or the way they behave, but this dislike is not strong enough to make them willing to change. Instead, they avoid being around people who are different, especially those whom they admire. Kathy is overweight but doesn't want to diet. Her best friends are mostly overweight or girls who don't push Kathy to change. Kathy refuses to be around girls who enjoy exercising, are diet conscious, or thin.

- They believe their way is the only right way.

It is difficult for these people to be with those who

don't conform to their way of thinking or acting. Such individuals want to control, change, and confront, and they usually will create an atmosphere of nonacceptance. They just don't understand why others can't "see the light" and conform.

Prepare your children to accept differences

When we learn to accept others as they are and appreciate our differences, our lives become unbelievably enriched. Differences are an important part of who we are. Paul talks about believers as different parts of the body of Christ. In 1 Corinthians 12:12–27, he talks about the need for differences and cautions us about putting one another down for being different.

- God made us different.

Each of us is designed and known by God, even before our birth (Ps. 139:13–16). We are God's handiwork, created in Christ Jesus for good works (Eph. 2:10). We are not intended to be identical. Everything God made is different from every other thing. Consider snowflakes and fingerprints, each one different from all the others.

- Be the best you can be.

We are to be stewards, good stewards, of what God has entrusted to us, including our selves, our ideas, and our choices (1 Cor. 3:21–4:8). Long before the world began, God planned for each of us to be conformed, not to each other, but to the Lord Jesus Christ. As God's children we have the Holy Spirit working in us to encourage us to strive for that ideal (Rom. 8:29).

- Accept who you are, change if you choose.

The first step toward accepting differences in others is to accept the differences (from others) in yourself. If your children truly accept themselves, they are less likely to feel criticized by differences in others.

Cora was shy in groups. Unlike most of her friends, she didn't like going to parties. She usually refused invitations and then felt left out when all her other friends attended. At first, Cora secretly thought that one of her friends should stay home with her.

When Cora acknowledged that her friends weren't wrong, they were just different, she decided to become more comfortable in large groups. She began working on her shyness, and within six months, she actually learned to enjoy herself at a party. Cora learned not to criticize her friends for being different but to work on her own issue first (Matt. 7:1–5).

- Draw on the strengths of others to make you better.

When discussing the body of Christ in 1 Corinthians, Paul explains how the different parts work together to form the body. One member provides the hearing, one the seeing, one the smelling, and so on. Without the differences, the body would be deficient. With the differences, the body is perfect and whole.

Help your children practice accepting differences

Here are some suggestions to help your children develop the ability to accept and appreciate differences in others.

- Give each family member a sheet of paper with your family members' names written across the top. Instruct them to write five to 10 words under each name that describe that person. Allow each family member to share his or her description of you. Share what you wrote under your own name. Then have each person share about someone else. Do this until all of the lists have been read. Discuss how each of you is different and how this helps the family as a whole.

- Give family members a sheet of paper that has a list of 15 characteristics. Examples include: cheerful, patient, caring, task-oriented, playful, serious, thrifty, generous, cautious, adventuresome, shy, bold, thoughtful, quiet, gregarious, talkative, and procrastinating. Discuss each one. When is it a nice characteristic? When do you appreciate it? Why do you appreciate it? Is it ever irritating to you? When? Why?

If you talk long enough, you will find that each characteristic can be terrific and terrible, depending on your point of view and the situation. Do this several times using different characteristics to teach your children to see both sides of a difference rather than just one.

- Ask your children to tell about their friends and the ways they are different. Encourage discussion about how differences can enrich their lives.

- Tell your children about friends you have that are different from you. Discuss what you have learned from them, why you appreciate them and their differences, and how your life is different (better) because you know them.

Teaching Kids to Handle Confrontation Productively

When someone confronts Nicole, she dissolves into tears and retreats. Rose argues. Lonnie gets angry. Jasper listens and discusses the differences in opinions or perspectives.

If Marlene needs to confront someone, she gets a stomachache. Agnes avoids that person. Todd does it right away to get it over with. Ross thinks the situation over and carefully plans what he will say before he approaches the person.

People handle disagreements in a number of

ways. Some are successful; some are disastrous. The way your children deal with disagreements and confrontations depends a great deal on how you have approached them in your family.

There are different types of disagreements and different ways to handle them. If someone's opinion is different from yours, you may discuss or debate the opinion. However, unless their opinion has an impact on your life and choices, you may not need to resolve the difference. Instead, you can agree to disagree. If the other person's opinions, wishes, needs, or ideas are different from yours and have an impact on your choices, you need to resolve the issue to a mutually agreeable solution as best you can.

There are even times when you may need to confront someone because of a disagreement. For example:

• When you are justifiably (in your mind) annoyed, displeased, or angry.

After being asked several times not to do so, Louise has "borrowed" Marie's clothes again without permission. Marie is justified in confronting Louise.

If you are angry with someone, it is important that you resolve the problem. This may involve going to the person, explaining what is wrong from your perspective, and listening to the other person's side of the story. It's called confrontation. Jesus instructed us to take the initiative to confront our friends and families, forgive them, and resolve issues that are problems in our relationships before we come to worship God (Matt. 5:23–24).

- When someone isn't treating you right.

When you believe someone isn't treating you in a respectful, courteous, or fair manner, you may need to confront that person. Letting someone know you are upset or unhappy starts the process of resolving the situation.

Sometimes when we tell others that we feel we're not being treated properly, we discover that our expectations are unrealistic and need to be revised.

One of the important aspects of confrontation is being able to see the other side of the coin. Often when we are offended by someone, we fail to realize that we may be offending them also. Sharing how you are feeling gives the other person a chance to describe how your behavior has affected him or her. It's an opportunity for the two of you to resolve the issues and ask for the Holy Spirit's guidance as you follow Paul's admonition to "bear with each other and forgive whatever grievances you may have against one another. Forgive as the Lord forgave you" (Col. 3:13).

- When you see someone doing something harmful.

Sometimes your children will see friends behaving in ways that are harmful to themselves or others. Encourage your children to confront their friends, describe the questionable actions, and encourage them to make changes in their ideas or behaviors. They may not always be grateful for what your children say, agree with your children's opinions, or make changes. But as friends, your children have a responsibility to provide such feedback because they care. The apostle Paul writes about confronting those who are doing things against God's standards. The purpose of confrontation is not to criticize but to restore and help the person and strengthen the relationship (1 Tim. 5:20; Gal. 6:1).

Understand why people aren't comfortable with confrontation

Many people are not comfortable with being confronted or with confronting others because they hold some misconceptions.

- Real friends don't disagree.

If your children believe that friends never disagree, they certainly will not be comfortable with confrontation. They won't acknowledge their feelings when they are upset or feel abused. They won't be skilled in standing up for their convictions.

- Nice people only say nice things.

People who only say nice things are not honest all

of the time. Most of us have negative feelings and don't always agree with the opinions, ideas, choices, and behaviors of others. If your children are afraid that confrontation means their friends won't think they are *nice*, you need to help your children redefine *nice*.

- Confrontation is only done in anger.

If your children only confront when they have had enough or are angry enough, the confrontation probably doesn't accomplish much. Confrontation works best when people are calm, have thought things through, and are willing to work at a relationship.

Prepare your children to productively handle confrontation

Confrontation is a process, and to be done productively, it requires skills. When talking with your children about confrontation, help them understand the process.

- Be clear about why you are confronting someone.

When Lazarus died, Jesus came to his house in Bethany and was greeted by Lazarus' sister, Martha. She confronted Jesus. "If only you had been here," she cried. "Lazarus wouldn't have died!" Martha wanted Jesus to know she believed in His power to heal. She trusted Him, but she was devastated by the death of her brother. She was disappointed, maybe even angry, that Jesus hadn't come in time to save her brother (John 11:1–44).

It is important that when there is a problem in a relationship, your children recognize that resolving it will strengthen the relationship. Confrontation just to prove superiority, to get one's way, to criticize, or to dominate is not appropriate and probably will not resolve anything.

- Be clear about what you want.

When Paul confronted the Corinthian Christians about their unacceptable behavior, he was very clear about what he wanted them to do and what changes he wanted them to make in their lives (1 Cor. 1:10–17; 5:1–6:8).

Disagreeing just to disagree is not helpful. Confrontation is appropriate when it's used to resolve an issue, reach a compromise, request a certain form of treatment, or encourage someone to make a life change. Before your children confront, they need to be clear about what they want to happen as a result of the confrontation. Then they can check their expectations and make sure they are realistic and reasonable.

- Decide when to confront.

When Nathan went to confront King David, I am sure he carefully chose the time and place to deliver God's message (2 Sam. 12:1–7).

Confrontation works best when done privately. It should not be done in the heat of an emotional outburst, but it should be carefully planned. It is important to choose a time to confront the person when he or she will be receptive and willing to listen. A confrontation when either party is angry, tired, pressed for time, or feeling ill is usually not productive.

- Choose your words.

The best way to confront someone is to avoid making accusations or beginning statements with the word *you*. Instead, tell the other person how you feel, what you think, and what you want. Begin your sentences with *I*. It is also helpful to start the conversation by affirming the relationship, describing the problem, sharing your feelings, and asking for what you want. The following is an example.

> *I value our friendship. Even though I am afraid this may upset you, I need to talk with you because I believe that we have a problem.*

> *When you _____ (describe a behavior such as "tease me in front of my friends"), I feel _____ (describe how you feel: "unloved," "left out," "embarrassed").*

> *What I would like is for you to _____*

_____ *(describe the desired behavior).*

Be sure to end by again affirming the relationship and telling the person how much you value him or her.

Paul was an expert at affirming the relationship. He would start his letters to the churches with affirmations. *"I thank God for you in my prayers"* (1 Cor. 1:4).

Then Paul would confront the problem. *"There are a few things we need to talk about ..."* (1 Cor. 1:10ff).

Paul would follow the confrontation with another affirmation. *"Oh, and greet one another and I love you"* (1 Cor. 16:22–24).

Help your children learn to handle confrontation productively

Here are some suggestions to help you teach your children to handle confrontation.

- Write 10 to 12 situations in which it would be appropriate to confront someone on index cards. Shuffle the cards. Have your children draw a card and role play the confrontation. (You could Play the person being confronted.) After each role play, discuss how it felt to confront, to be confronted, and ways the confrontation might have been handled differently. In some cases, ask your children to repeat the role play using a different confrontational style.

- Watch a family situation comedy on television together. Be on the alert for confrontations. Make notes. Discuss each confrontation after the show. What was the reason for the confrontation? How was it handled? Was it done in private? Were "I" statements made? What was the result of the confrontation? How could it have been handled differently/better?

- Share stories about times when you were confronted and how you felt. If the confrontation was successful, share that. If it was not successful, share why you felt it was not. Discuss how you would have preferred the matter to have been handled.

- Invite your children to talk about issues they feel need to be confronted in the next few days. Discuss different ways to handle the confrontation. Follow up with your children to see how the issues were resolved.

Teaching Kids to Build Positive Relationships

In the last chapter and the first part of this one, we have discussed several different aspects of communication and relating. These apply to all friendships and relationships, including those in the family. In addition, your kids will need other skills as they build positive friendships and move into dating and more serious relationships with the opposite sex. Let's look at a few of these.

Get to know one another

Perry overheard his son talking with a friend on the phone. Ray was discussing a new girl in school. Apparently she had just arrived, was gorgeous, and Ray was planning to ask her out. He was already thinking about going steady. They hadn't even met yet.

It is essential in the friendship-building process that people get to know one another. This means knowing more about them than how they look. Teach your children how to get to know other people. When they become teenagers, they need to be skilled at asking questions, listening, watching, and observing others. Getting to know someone involves learning how and what they think, their opinions and history, their fears and dreams, their plans and expectations. Therefore, a lot of sharing and discussion is necessary for people to be able to say they truly "know" someone.

Spend time working together

One way to learn about others is to work together on projects, homework assignments, chores, or even to play together on a team or in a one-on-one game. When your kids participate in these activities, they see how others approach challenges, deal with frustrations, control emotions, enjoy achievements, solve problems, behave under various conditions, function in a partnership, contribute to the final outcome, and communicate instructions. These activities are wonderful for building friendships (or for discovering irreconcilable differences). Working on projects together provides opportunities to negotiate which person will take charge and to develop cooperative skills.

Get rid of unrealistic expectations

Building good relationships also requires that neither person clings to unrealistic expectations. Unrealistic expectations come in many areas of relationships. Teach your children to recognize unmet expectations. The clues include disappointment or feeling hurt or angry. Encourage your kids always to ask "What did I expect/want to happen that didn't?" Then evaluate the expectation. Was it reasonable? Was it realistic? Was it shared with the other person ahead of time? Or was it a secret expectation? Unrealistic or nonverbalized expectations cause problems in relationships and must be avoided.

Invest in each other's life

Another way to develop strong relationships is

to consciously invest in each other's lives. This involves caring about what happens, doing what you can to support each other, choosing to do things to please each other, expressing the value placed on the relationship, helping each other when appropriate, and finding a good balance of giving and taking.

To discover what the other person wants and what the goals of the relationship are requires emotional energy, time, and caring. But it doesn't stop there. Both individuals must then deliberately seek to encourage, assist, motivate, and support the other person in those endeavors. This process builds intimacy and depth in relationships.

Treat one another with respect

Belittling, using sarcasm, teasing, snapping at, interrupting, refusing to listen to, and taking advantage of others break up relationships. Your teenagers probably know this, but they may not realize that these behaviors are even more hurtful in an intimate relationship. Why do we often behave our worst in our most important relationships? We treat family members in ways we would not treat dates. We treat dates in ways we would not treat friends. We even sometimes treat friends in ways we would not treat acquaintances. We shouldn't expect those who care about us to excuse us and accept our worst behaviors.

Teach your children to treat everyone with

respect and love, especially family members and friends (including dates). This is so important that Paul writes in Romans 13:8–10 that if we were to live with love toward others, we would fulfill all aspects of the Law. In other words, if we acted lovingly at all times, we would not offend or hurt others or break any of God's Laws for us. Unfortunately, most of us still need work in this area.

Have other friends

Helen is one of those teenagers who wants only one friend at a time. When she becomes friends with someone new, she drops her "old" friend and focuses exclusively on the new friend. Her parents have noticed that she has transferred that perspective into her dating relationship. She started dating Walter and stopped calling her best girlfriend. Helen says Walter is the only friend she needs. She wants Walter always to be ready to go out with her, listen to her, play games with her, study with her, walk to school with her, eat lunch with her, and in essence, spend all his free time with her.

That's too great an expectation to put on any one person. Helen needs to have several friends and appreciate each for their differences and the ways they enrich her life. Unless Helen learns this important lesson, she may continue to be possessive, jealous, and clinging. Eventually, this will drive Walter away, as well as countless others in the future. Having many friends helps your kids avoid developing an unhealthy dependency on one person, a desperate need to cling to that person.

When I look at the different types of men Jesus called to be His disciples, I see great variety. There were outspoken, quiet, ambitious, and helpful men. Some were fishermen; one was a tax collector. When Jesus developed a closer relationship with three of His disciples (Peter, James, and John), each man was unique from the others.

Build on Christian principles

When friendships and relationships are based on Christian principles, chances are good they will succeed and be healthy. Your children can improve their relational skills by treating others as parts of God's family and valued members of the body of Christ, striving to support others in their spiritual growth and development, and relating to others in the spirit of Christian love.

Codependent relationships are a hot topic these days. Encourage your children to develop healthy two-way relationships that are not built on one person's dependency on the other. In a codependent relationship, there is a tendency to love for the wrong reasons, to do things for the other person only to gain acceptance and affirmation.

Paul describes in 1 Cor. 13:4–8 a godly model of a loving relationship:

Love is patient, love is kind. It does not envy, it does not boast, it is not proud. It is not rude, it is not self-seeking, it is not easily angered, it keeps no record of wrongs. Love does not delight in evil but rejoices with the truth. It always protects, always trusts, always hopes, always perseveres. Love never fails.

In a healthy love relationship, the other person is valued. There is a desire to do things to please your partner. But there is also a healthy self-respect that allows both giving and receiving. Teach your teens to develop relationships in which they feel secure and are able to express themselves. They should not be afraid of losing the relationship because they say or do the wrong thing. They should not let themselves be taken advantage of all of the time.

Encourage your children to work on their relational skills so their dating relationships will be rewarding.

5

ARE THEY READY
FOR THE
DYNAMICS?

Marian answered the phone, heard a familiar voice ask for Russ, covered the mouthpiece, and called her son. "It's Cindy," she mouthed quietly.

"Hi," Russ said, smiling into the telephone as he talked, completely at ease with the call.

Marian was not. "I just can't get used to having girls call the house," Marian confessed to her friend Sylvia. "It doesn't seem right. When I was 14, I would never have called a boy. I had to wait for him to call me."

"I know," Sylvia said gently, "but things are different now. It's okay for girls to do the calling. Besides, who says boys have to be risk rejection all the time by doing the asking and the calling?"

Today, teens of either sex may call the other. Both sexes may risk initial rejection. Both boys and girls must learn to deal with the dynamics of dating. In some cases, your kids have things to learn. In other cases, you may have some learning and accepting to do in order to live with the new dimensions in relationships.

Telephoning the Opposite Sex

"I feel like an answering service," Marian complained. "Since Russ turned 14, the phone never seems to stop ringing. Usually it's for him, and more than half the time it's a girl calling. I get upset a lot over the phone issue, not just because he spends so much time on it, but because it's a constant disruption. Often I can't call home when I'm out because the line is busy. I can't make my own calls without asking Russ to get off the phone. And that 'ring,' 'ring,' 'ring' all the time!"

One problem as a parent of teenagers is the phone. Most kids love to talk on the phone. Many parents have made telephone adjustments such as adding a second line or a call holding service. This ensures you can always get through when you call home. Other parents even get their teenagers a separate phone line that rings in their rooms.

If you wait until your teenagers want to spend all their free time on the phone or until the number of calls annoys or upsets you, it is long past time to discuss the phone's use. Discuss and decide the limitations that will be set. The following are some examples:

"Phone calls must wait until after homework is done."

"No calls, in or out, during dinner."

"Phone calls are limited to 15 minutes."

"Never use both phone lines at the same time. Always leave one open so parents can call home."

"No calls, in or out, after bedtime."

Involve your kids in the discussion and decision making about the phone's use. They can also help decide the consequences for violating the rules.

Teach your kids to be sensitive to the home situation of the kids they are calling. Encourage them to find out the phone rules in their friends' homes so they won't upset their friends' parents. A teenager who asks when a convenient time to call back would be earns more appreciation from the parent on the other end than the teen who says, "I'll call back," and does so every 15 minutes.

The nice thing about your kids talking on the phone is that you know where they are and that they are physically safe and protected. For kids, it is a way to spend time with their friends even though they are at home. Phones are great! However, discuss with your kids that phone conversations can be very different from talking face to face. For some people, it is easier to open up on the phone than in person. Therefore, during long phone conversations your kids may learn more about someone than they might have in a couple of hours together. Phone conversations also can easily become more intimate than appropriate unless you set some limits. Help your kids learn to consider their telephone relationships and conversations as a part of their lives—a part that should be lived in a manner pleasing to God. Consider what Psalm 19:14 says about our conversations:

May the words of my mouth and the meditation of my heart be pleasing in your sight, O LORD my Rock and my Redeemer.

Asking for a Date

"There ought to be a class in how to ask for a date," Jeremy said, laughing. "I remember the agony I suffered when I was a kid, longing to ask a girl out, not knowing how, and afraid she would say no. I wonder how many dates I missed because I was too afraid to even ask."

Asking someone for a date is risky. There's always a chance the response will be no. For a long time, the boy/man asked the girl/woman for a date. The males assumed the risk of rejection. Today, more and more girls initiate the dating invitation and experience the risk of rejection.

Talk with your kids about the process of asking someone for a date. They can increase the chance for success if they find out what the other person likes to do. Then they can invite that person to such an activity. Inviting a boy to go out with a group instead of on a one-on-one activity for the first date, may increase the chance of a yes. Group activities are less threatening and do not necessarily imply a desire for a long-term commitment.

Only practice will improve your kids' asking skills. To practice the process of asking, your kids could invite friends of both sexes to do fun things together without the expectation of romantic involvement. The potential for a painful rejection lessens significantly when the emotional involvement is minimal.

Teach your teens to practice a little self-disclosure when they ask someone for a date. They can preface a request for a date with a personal disclosure such as, "I've wanted to get to know you better for a long time;" "I would like you for a friend;" or "I'm a little shy about asking you out, but I would really like to get to know you and see if we might become friends."

Asking for a date can be done in person, by telephone, or even in a written note. Remind your kids that if they're going to ask in person, do it privately, not in front of a group. Encourage your teens to use different ways to ask someone out and find the one that works best.

As always, there is a chance that your teens will be rejected. Help them accept that possibility and understand that a no is not a reason to feel devastated or embarrassed. There is nothing wrong with being caught caring. A desire to go out with someone is a gift of acceptance you give that person. The individual usually appreciates the interest, even if he or she doesn't accept the invitation.

Planning Special Dates

Twenty-two-year-old Stella was telling her younger brother, Lee, about her dating experiences. "My favorite dating partner was Anthony," she said as her eyes sparkled with the memories. "He knew how to make a date really exciting. I always felt I was special and that what we were doing was an adventure. Sometimes when I told my girlfriends about one of our dates, I discovered that I couldn't describe why it had been so special. Anthony just had a way about him that made even simple activities wonderful.

"Once he picked me up and told me we were going to have the best hamburger in the world. He said the place wasn't fancy, but he'd never had a better burger. He said that he hadn't shared this discovery with anyone else, but he wanted me to experience it. We drove to a small burger place in Los Angeles called 'Tommy's.' Sure enough, it was the best hamburger I ever tasted. Although the place really is very famous and celebrities stop in for hamburgers, I think part of the reason the burgers tasted so good was Anthony's enthusiasm and the anticipation I felt at being taken to this unique place.

"When you come right down to it, it was just a hamburger-and-fries date. It shouldn't have been a big deal, but

Anthony could make anything special."

Help your teens make their dates interesting and exciting. Doing something different, meeting special people, listening to a terrific motivational speaker, visiting an art gallery, even going to the library can be unique experiences. Your teenagers have to find what's unusual about the activity, the artist, the author, or the location and share this excitement of discovery with their dates. Then there is a good chance the date will be terrific.

Dates don't need to be expensive to be enjoyable. Encourage your teenagers to use creativity and imagination when planning dates. A picnic on a perfect day, a drive to see an unusual site—these can make wonderful memories.

Stella remembered another date with Anthony. "He loved to take pictures and had sighted this unusual, old tree on a bare hill. He imagined it at sunset with the sky darkening and the light outlining the branches and the bare hill. He went back several times and finally caught the light just perfectly for his picture. The sight was spectacular. He had the picture copied, blown up to an 8" × 10" size, framed, and wrapped. At the time, I knew nothing about this.

"One day in the late afternoon, he picked me up and told me we were going to see the most wonderful view. He drove me to the hill, spread a blanket on the ground in a perfect position to catch the sun setting behind the tree, and then told me to watch carefully. We talked for about an hour

and then he began describing how he had first seen this tree, imagined it at sunset, and come back several times to catch the moment as he had pictured it. As the sun began to set, we held our breath and watched the picture form. It was beautiful. I was glad that Anthony had shared the experience with me. When he dropped me off at home, he gave me the framed picture. 'So you will be able to remember this experience forever,' he said. I was speechless."

Careful planning is the key to a unique date. Your teens can make a lasting impression if they conduct themselves with style and class.

Breaking Up

One of the steps in the teenage dating dance is breaking up. It happens in most relationships. The stories of a couple who met in junior high school, became friends, began dating in high school, married, went to college, and celebrated their 50th wedding anniversary are few and far between. Most people either break up with or are broken up with several times during their teen years.

Breaking up is hard—usually for both parties.

The decision to end a relationship is not usually easy. The couple may realize the relationship is not working, or it's restrictive, or it's codependent, or it isn't satisfying. These realizations usually result in a desire to end the relationship. On the other hand, the couple may be afraid that if this relationship ends, there may not be another one to replace it right away. That intervening time could be very lonely. Ending a relationship is often put off because one person doesn't want to hurt his or her partner or doesn't know how to call it off.

Before your teens get into serious dating relationships, discuss the issues involved in ending relationships. Help them learn how to evaluate relationships. This evaluation is an important part of deciding if a relationship is one your kids want to continue. One good way to evaluate a relationship is to make a list of what one is receiving and what one is giving in the relationship.

The awkwardness of breaking off a relationship comes from a lack of skill in saying good-bye and a desire to avoid unpleasantness and pain. Even if both parties are secretly ready to end the relationship, it is instinctive to feel rejected, which causes the one who didn't institute the break up to feel hurt.

There is probably no right way to end a relationship or save a partner from pain. Teach your kids to make every effort to preserve the dignity and the respect of both parties.

Teens who have practiced the communication skills described in earlier chapters will be better able to confront a partner with the end of a relationship.

"I still care about you as a friend, but I don't want to go out only with you."

"I think you're a great person, but I want you as a friend and not as a dating partner."

These things are not easy to say, but they are direct ways to both affirm the person and dissolve the dating relationship.

Dealing with Rejection

Rejection is a complicated issue. It always feels so personal. When people reject your ideas, suggestions, or invitations, you usually feel as if they are rejecting you. This may be true, but quite often it is not. When someone pulls away from a relationship, it is usually a painful experience of rejection. When a partner breaks up with your teen, the result can be devastating.

Understand rejection

• The timing may be wrong.

Susie was just getting over a relationship when Trent asked her out. She wasn't ready to date anyone else just yet. She said no. Susie wasn't ruling Trent out as a possible date forever, she wasn't even rejecting Trent as a person. Susie was rejecting the idea of going out with anyone other than the boy who had broken up with her.

Paul was not open to going out with Eileen when she asked him. His grades weren't too good, and he desperately needed to study every night to make good grades on his final exams. Paul needed a scholarship for college, and he wouldn't get one unless he crammed for finals every minute he wasn't in school. He wasn't rejecting Eileen; he just didn't have time to date.

Virginia broke off a dating relationship with her boyfriend when they graduated from high school. She was going to college and didn't feel she ought to continue a relationship to which she was no longer emotionally committed. She wasn't ready to settle down, get engaged, and consider marriage.

When Lawrence's dad died, he felt as if he needed to withdraw from his close friends, including his girlfriend. He wasn't in a good emotional state to continue the relationship at that time.

- The initial invitation may not be appropriate or the personal preferences may not match.

Ruth liked classical music and turned Ramon down when he invited her to a country music festival. Had the request been for something else, Ruth might have said yes.

Dwayne was trying to lose 10 pounds to qualify for his favorite sport at school. He refused Paula's invitation for an ice cream sundae social at church. He loved ice cream and knew he wouldn't be able to resist the temptation.

Bethany and Brian had been going together for a couple months. At first they enjoyed being together so much that they took turns adjusting to each other's desires and preferences. After a while, they realized that they didn't have a lot in common. It seemed that one of them was always giving in to the other. Finally, Brian broke off the relationship.

- The level of interaction may be the issue.

Emily and Brett had been friends for a couple years. Emily had always had a secret fantasy that the friendship would turn into something more. When Brett broke up with his latest girlfriend, Emily risked asking Brett about the possibility of their going out together. Brett, who had never thought of Emily as a potential girlfriend, gently refused. Emily was embarrassed and felt totally rejected. She withdrew from Brett and gave up the good friendship they had had.

What Emily failed to understand was that Brett wasn't rejecting her as a person, he valued her friendship. He was rejecting her offer of moving the friendship into the romance arena.

Your kids must learn to identify what is being rejected instead of immediately personalizing the rejection and becoming devastated. If timing is the issue, a request at a different time may be accepted. If the activity is inappropriate, a different request may have different results. If the level of interaction is the problem, then your teens must decide if they are willing to maintain the current relationship even if their desires for a different relationship cannot be realized.

Flora and Jared had been dating casually for three months. They had each passed their 17th birthday when Flora began to talk about getting married as soon as they graduated from high school. Jared was not ready for marriage in the near future. He had college plans and ideas about going into military service. Because she could not convince Jared to consider getting engaged, Flora broke up with him.

Cope with rejection

Everyone must cope with rejection. Yet few are prepared for it. Here are some helpful suggestions for your kids.

- Acknowledge the pain.

Rejection hurts. No one gets up in the morning, stretches, and goes out in search of a rejection experience. In fact, we do our best to avoid rejection. When someone says no, it hurts. Rather than denying the hurt, the first step in coping is to acknowledge the pain.

- Do something physical.

Believe it or not, doing something physical, preferably a strenuous activity, helps work through some of the emotional pain of rejection, which often is experienced as physical discomfort. An upset stomach, chest pain, shortness of breath, and headaches can be physical symptoms of the emotional distress caused by rejection. These physical symptoms are triggered as the body mobilizes the stress response to answer the emotional distress. Heavy physical activity works out some of the stress response and will temporarily reduce the physical pain.

- Be with other people.

When your kids are rejected, they may be tempted to hide from people, nurse the pain, and experience self-pity. Help them resist this temptation and force themselves to be around other people. Your teens could go visit a friend, spend an evening with the family, attend a young people's event at church, or find ways to interact with others.

- Seek affirmation.

Find ways to affirm your teens following a rejection experience. Hugs from family members, good times with friends, talking out the rejection with friends, or reminders of past accomplishments and good qualities are ways of affirming your kids' lives.

Remind your teens that their worth as people is not dependent on acceptance by the opposite sex. We are worthy because God considered each of us to be worth the sacrifice of His Son on the cross. We were chosen by God to be members of His eternal family (John 15:15–17; Eph. 1:4–6; 1 Peter 1:18–19; 1 John 4:19).

- Discover what was rejected.

When the time is appropriate, it may be helpful to discover what was rejected. Was the request for a date rejected because of timing or appropriateness? Or was the rejection a result of the level of interaction? If your kids discover why they were rejected, then appropriate decisions can be made about what to do next. Perhaps behaviors need to change so there will be acceptance in future relationships. Perhaps the reasons for the rejection reflect poorly on the people who did the rejecting and not on your teens.

- Learn from the rejection.

After a time, encourage your teens to identify what they learned from the rejection. Should they not rush into relationships? Do they need to behave in a particular way such as being more open, honest, or caring? Were they too possessive or jealous? Should they be less critical or passive?

Use each rejection experience to help your teens develop character and prepare for the next relationship.

Dating Ethics

Encourage your children to maintain good dating ethics. If they are going steady, there is a definite commitment not to date anyone else. It is not appropriate to share with others what has been told in confidence between the partners. Honesty is essential in a good relationship. Courtesy toward one another is desirable. Put the "golden rule" into practice in dating relationships to ensure that both parties behave in a positive manner toward one another.

You can do a lot to prepare your children for the dynamics of the dating process. Remember how painful some of the lessons are when learned in the dating arena? Help your children avoid that pain as much as possible and help them prepare for positive dating relationships.

WHAT ARE THE
DATING RULES?

"Why are there always so many rules?" 15-year-old Cynthia groaned in disgust as her parents were discussing whether to allow her to date alone. *"I'm almost grown up, but every time I get to do something different, there's always a new set of rules to follow."*

"You're right, Cyn," her dad said gently. *"That's the way things are in life. When I get new responsibilities at work, there are new guidelines and parameters I have to obey. When Mom buys a new appliance, there are instructions she must follow to make it work properly. Rules, guidelines, or instructions, they're just a part of life we all must live with. That's because for every choice, for every behavior, there is a consequence. Consequences for poor choices or bad decisions are not pleasant. To experience the best results, we have to make good decisions. That's where the rules come in. They help us know what the good decisions are."*

"Maybe," Cynthia admitted reluctantly. *"But it doesn't feel good. It feels like I'm being treated like a child all the time."*

"I know. Sometimes I feel that way too," her dad confided.

Attraction Develops Quickly

Guidelines or rules are necessary in most aspects of life. They are critical when bad or wrong decisions bring serious consequences. Poor decisions in relationships can have hurtful and serious consequences, which makes good guidelines an essential part of the process.

God made us physical and sexual beings. He gave us the gift of enjoying the attraction, interaction, and excitement of bonding together through physical intimacy. And when God surveyed all of creation, including us sexual human beings, the evaluation was "It was very good" (Gen. 1:31). We have been given custody of our physical selves, including our sexuality, and we will be held accountable for the decisions we make.

Attraction between a boy and a girl (or even a man and a woman) can develop quickly. There can be an appreciation for the outward appearance that triggers the interest. Or there can be a moment of emotional or mental connectedness that creates an emotional attraction. Attraction often starts with a physical response, a heightened awareness of the other person, a desire to touch, to belong, and even to possess or own the other person. Soon thoughts of the focus of the attraction intrude into all other thoughts, becoming the most important thoughts.

As soon as your teens act on the attraction, a relationship is set into motion and often continues to move of its own accord. If there is a reciprocal attraction or interest, the relationship can progress amazingly quickly, unless you take conscious steps to slow the development. Because of the immediate reward and satisfaction of the longings your teens experience, physical intimacy often develops early in a relationship. This is one reason to slow the relationship's growth.

At first, just thinking of the person is satisfying. Long hours are spent daydreaming or writing name combinations (*Bob loves Rita* or *Mrs. Robert Manning*). But daydreaming won't satisfy for long. The next step may be spending time with the person, even if it is in a group. Soon that won't be enough. The couple will spend long hours talking (in person or on the phone). Going out together only satisfies for so long before hand holding is a must. The move from holding hands to sexual exploration can be incredibly quick, taking only a matter of minutes, or it can be deliberately delayed depending on your teens' standards. Understand, however, that the progression is a natural one, a powerful one, and one that cannot be left unchecked.

Everyone Is Vulnerable

"When I walked in on my 16-year-old and her boyfriend making out on the couch last week, I was shocked," Maggie confessed to her pastor. "Shelley was brought up to be a nice Christian girl. I never thought I would have to worry about her getting physically involved with a boy before marriage."

"Everyone is vulnerable, Maggie," the pastor stated gently. "Even Christian young people."

That's very true.

According to psychologist Robert Stromberg, there are three elements of relationships that we all long for: passion, commitment, and intimacy. When all three elements are present and in equal proportion, the relationship is healthy and satisfying. However, when one or more of these elements is lacking, we feel unfulfilled and unsatisfied. Then we become vulnerable to developing a relationship that will provide the missing element.

Intimacy includes being open and honest about who we are and allowing another to see us as we really are. Because we are complex persons, there are many levels of intimacy. Most protect their inner self with masks and barriers that keep others from seeing everything. When a close relationship develops, the barriers are removed, one at a time, until there are few secrets. While intimacy is scary, it is also a fulfilling element of relationships when the openness results in acceptance by the other.

Intimacy needs are first met by same-sex friends. This is evident as your kids form "best-friend" relationships in childhood or their preteen years. Teens continue to have friends and even best friends, as do adults, but the satisfaction level diminishes as the desire for intimacy with the opposite sex develops.

Teens who understand the need for intimacy can choose to develop open and honest friendships with several friends of both sexes. A proper understanding of the need for intimacy will help your teens wait to fulfill all their intimacy needs until they are old enough to make a life commitment with a member of the opposite sex.

Commitment involves belonging in a special way reserved for the two people in the relationship. Usually the commitment implies exclusivity and a promise to remain in the relationship even through tough times. Commitment means the couple will work through problems and stick together against others. Because commitment satisfies the need to belong, it is essential to most of us.

The need for commitment is first met through participation in clubs, sports teams, or other self-defined groups. A commitment to be best friends with someone of the same sex is also satisfying during your children's early years. However, "belonging" with a member of the opposite sex can be more exciting and desirable, so teens begin to long for a romantic relationship.

Encourage your teens to meet their need to belong by focusing on participation in the body of Christ, Christians who choose to live according to God's standards. Commitments made to groups of other teens who are working for higher causes, such as short-term mission trips, community outreach, evangelism, or social justice issues can help meet some of your kids' needs to commit. However, your teens need to acknowledge that in most cases commitment to other relationships and causes is not as satisfying as being in a committed relationship with a member of the opposite sex. Total fulfillment of the need to belong, to experience commitment with another person, is reserved for the marriage relationship.

Passion is the physical element of the relationship, the chemistry, the excitement, the sexual longing, or the desire to mate. As children pass through adolescence into young adulthood, their physical changes create an awareness and longing for physical satisfaction that can be present in a relationship with the opposite sex.

Children's initial interest in passion is mainly intellectual. They want to know what the physical side of love is all about. While there may be some physical exploration, it is usually limited. The curiosity remains and grows until there is actual sexual involvement and satisfaction. However, you need to help your teens understand that choices in this area have serious consequences. They need to be made with biblical principles in mind.

There comes a time when parents, families, and even same-sex friends are not able to fully meet these three needs your teens experience. They become vulnerable to developing relationships with the opposite sex that progress too quickly. Your kids must understand these needs and be willing to respond to these needs in godly ways.

Time Alone Together Can Be Dangerous

The more time a couple spends alone together, the more intimate their relationship tends to become. Therefore, it is wise to limit the amount of time your teens spend totally alone with their dates. (Some of the books listed in the appendix can help discuss this topic with your teens, specifically *Too Close Too Soon* by Jim A. Talley and Bobbie Reed.)

A couple that spends six hours together (from 6 p.m. to midnight) is likely to become more physically intimate than one that spends two hours together from 7 p.m. to 9 p.m. Unless the couple is already physically involved, they usually catch up on what's happened since they last saw each other and participate in an activity (watch a television show, listen to music, or eat a meal). The longer a couple is alone together at one time, the more physically aware they may become of each other. They may become more tempted to meet their physical needs and longings. Maintaining their standards while alone together draws on your kids' moral "batteries." Accumulated time alone together discharges those batteries, and they can run down or fail. Time apart can help your teens reflect on their commitment to live according to God's standards and, therefore, recharge their moral "batteries."

Psychologist Jim Talley believes couples that accumulate 300 hours alone together may cross over the line of physical and sexual involvement. Although not an arbitrary or absolute figure, use this number as a guideline to discuss limits with your teens. It is not difficult to accumulate 300 hours.

Dennis and Judy are both 15. They are going steady. They walk to and from school together each day and spend an hour and a half alone at one of their houses working on homework. (That's 2 ½ hours a day, five days a week, or 12 ½ hours a week.) They are allowed to date on Friday and Saturday nights but have to be in by 11 p.m. If they go out alone and spend five hours a date, that increases the hours to 22 ½ hours a week. Dennis and Judy usually spend either (or both) weekend afternoons together, which adds five to 10 hours to the weekly total. In 10 to 12 weeks, they could easily reach 300 hours alone together! Dennis and Judy's progression toward sexual intimacy speeds up when the time they spend together at groups (twice a week at church) and talking on the phone (nightly) is added to the total.

To slow down your kids' progression toward sexual intimacy, limit the time they spend alone with their boyfriends/girlfriends. It should be no more than two to four hours a week if that time is spent in secluded or unsupervised places (in the car, at home alone, etc.). Increase the time to eight to 10 hours as long as the extra hours are spent in public places (walking to and from school, playing tennis, picnics in the park, etc.). Try to restrict other time together to group activities.

Encourage your teens to chart the time they spend with their dates and see for themselves how it adds up. If they accept the fact that being alone together puts them in temptation's way, they may be more willing to work with you to keep their relationship under control. Remind them that God will provide a way out of a temptation (1 Cor. 10:13). Responsibly planning time alone together and controlling it is one way they can resist temptation.

Also consider how your teens spend their time with their dates. Three hours at the kitchen table playing Monopoly is less dangerous than three hours in a darkened living room watching a romantic movie or listening to romantic music. Encourage your teens to plan active dates, and activities in well-lighted rooms, to help themselves restrict their physical involvement.

The "safest" dates, those that build the relationship but are least likely to lead to premature sexual intimacy, are those with groups; those that occur during the daytime; those that involve physical activities such as sports; or those that are in public places. The more of these dates your teens have, the healthier the relationship is likely to become. These activities and settings encourage and develop other types of intimacy (emotional, mental, spiritual, recreational, and social) rather than just the physical.

Setting Standards Is Essential

Setting the standards for acceptable behaviors is an important aspect of preparing your teens to date. Because your teenagers will be alone, they must be the ones to accept the standards and enforce them. Before your teens begin to date alone, discuss with them the standards they need to set for their dates. This discussion needs to set limits on physical touching.

As you talk with your teens, discuss the reality that relationships include physical excitement, which is tempting to pursue and experience. But the problem arises when one level of physical touching becomes familiar and the next level of touching becomes the new exciting temptation. This means hugging and serious kissing on one date could pave the way for more intimate touching on subsequent dates. Your teens need to set limits early in the relationship to maintain an appropriate standard of dating behavior. Without standards, touching can progress to sexual intimacy very quickly.

As Christians, God's Holy Spirit accompanies us everywhere we go. Remind your teens that they need to be aware of the Holy Spirit's presence on their dates also. Then they can set standards that will help them maintain a Christian witness such as refusing to attend R-rated movies, break the law, experiment with drugs and/or alcohol, or permit unacceptable physical intimacy.

It is hard for your teens to stand up for their convictions on a date because they risk rejection for not going along with their dates' suggestions. That's why you need to discuss these issues long before your kids are ready to date. Then their convictions will be deeply ingrained and more difficult to ignore.

One dating rule you may establish is an appropriate age span for those your teens may date. The person they date as teens should not be significantly younger or older than they are. An older teen or someone who is out of high school may be more experienced and have expectations of physical involvement that are not acceptable for your teens. Older individuals probably have a much later curfew, or no curfew at all, and may put pressure on your teens to stay out later than allowed. There may be other pressures your teens do not need to be subjected to that could challenge their convictions beyond their abilities to stand firm.

On the other hand, if your teens are much older than the individuals they want to date, consider the same issues in reverse. You do not want your teen to tempt a younger person to disobey the dating rules set by the other parents.

You might also encourage your teens to date only those persons with similar faith and convictions. This provides more compatibility in the relationship, and both teens can help each other remain faithful to their convictions. This does not mean that just because the other teen believes the same as yours that there will be no temptations. There are no guarantees. But if both teens start off with the same beliefs, they are more likely to adhere to them.

To set standards, think through the various elements and aspects of relationships and decide where to draw the lines. Make these decisions before your teenagers begin dating. Although you want to influence the choices your teens make, you cannot make their choices for them. You must instruct, model, and help your children understand the consequences of making good and poor choices. Then constantly remember your children in your prayers. Trust that when temptation comes, the Holy Spirit will bring to their minds the decisions they have made and will give them the strength to stand by their convictions (John 14:26).

Being Accountable

Even though relationships can progress quickly and get out of control, the good news is that getting too involved physically is not "one big decision." Rather, it is a series of small decisions that lead to the final choice.

There is a story of a young man who went to his pastor because the night before he and his girlfriend had "gone too far" and his guilt was overwhelming.

"Pastor," he started out, "we didn't plan it. We never thought it would happen to us. We didn't want to do it. I guess the devil was just too strong for us. He made me do it."

The pastor nodded wisely and said, "Let me understand this. The devil called your girlfriend and asked for a date, right?"

"No," the young man replied thoughtfully. "No, I did that."

"Oh," the pastor continued. "Then the devil must have taken your girlfriend to that secluded restaurant with romantic music, candles, and private booths, right?"

"No," the young man admitted. "I did that."

"I see," the pastor said. "Then it must have been the devil who drove the car out to Make-Out Point after dinner."

The young man hung his head. "I did that too."

"Then the devil put his arm around your girlfriend?"

"No, I did."

"Then he must have been the one who began to undress your girlfriend?"

"No," the young man said sadly. *"I did that."*

Understanding that one becomes progressively involved by making a series of small choices is easier to see in retrospect than in the heat of the moment. Take the time to discuss these issues with your teens long before the sequence of decisions sweeps them away emotionally.

When your teens grasp this truth, they can better understand the wisdom of limiting time alone together, setting standards for acceptable behavior, and even the need to be accountable for their decisions.

You need to be your children's partner in the accountability aspect of dating, even though your kids may feel this is more like control. If your teens agree to chart their time alone with their dates and share the chart with you, this can help. When your teens agree to tell you what they have planned for the date, they will be more likely to plan appropriate and less tempting dates. Planning for the date also encourages your kids to actually *plan* rather than just "letting whatever happens, happen."

If your teens understand a curfew is part of being held accountable, they may be more willing to work with you rather than resist and argue for a later curfew.

Don't be surprised if your teens are reluctant to discuss their dates with you. Your children are beginning to pull away from you and establish their own independence. However, within limits, they may be willing to share with you or even ask your advice, especially if you listen patiently rather than respond with criticism.

Your kids need to understand the limits and the accountability are for their protection. You want the best relationships for them, and these guidelines are motivated by your love for them. This does not mean, however, that your teens will agree that your interest and your rules are acceptable for them.

Make your home a place where your kids like to bring their friends and you may have a place where your kids feel comfortable bringing their dates. Provide interesting table games, video games, and outside activities. Keep the freezer stocked with snacks you can prepare without much notice. Buy sodas on sale and maintain a good supply. Show your interest in the kids when they come over but learn to be nonintrusive. It is best to know where your kids are, and to have them at home, than to spend every evening worrying about them.

As you and your kids discuss the standards and the rules for dating, you will modify your relationship and move toward the counselor/friend interaction that characterizes the relationship between parent and adult child. While you still exercise some control over the consequences of failing to meet the established standards, you will gradually relinquish the decision-making to your kids as they move toward full adulthood.

Prayerfully approach this aspect of your child's development and ask God's blessing to do your best as a parent to train your children in the ways they ought to go (Prov. 22:6).

7

WHY WAIT
FOR SEXUAL
INTIMACY?

"I think it's probably much harder for our kids to remain chaste until marriage than it was for us when we were young," Oscar admitted. Others in the class nodded in agreement. Several parents had gathered for a six-week class in "Parenting Your Teen," and this week's session was about teen sexuality.

"I wish we could just lock them up for the next six or seven years and only let them out when they are old enough to make the right choices," Milly quipped facetiously. Some of the parents laughed understandingly.

Unfortunately, one of the critical areas parents face as they raise their children is helping them understand and make responsible choices about sexuality.

Reasons Kids Have Sex

"Knowing what can happen from having sex with different partners, how can kids ignore the possible conse-

quences and go ahead anyway? I just don't understand,"
one mother commented.

Many teens do become sexually active even though they know the possible consequences. There is usually a strong sense of "It won't happen to me" that relaxes their fears and allows the choice for involvement. Besides, there are many reasons that teens have sex, and only a few of them are physical. (See the appendix for more information on *Why Wait?* by Josh McDowell and Dick Day, a terrific resource for any parent who wants to understand this aspect of their teen's development and help them make wise choices.) This chapter provides only a brief discussion of the complex issues involved in teenage sexuality.

- "It's the next step."

As we have already seen in previous chapters, one level of physical intimacy leads to the next. As soon as one intimate action becomes familiar, the next "thrilling" intimacy is desired and achieved. Therefore, at some point, intercourse will be the next step, and some teens will proceed rather than draw the line. To help your teens avoid this decision, help them draw the line several steps before intercourse. In this way, they can exercise self-control before the choice is intercourse. The further back from intercourse the line is drawn, the less self-control will be required to say no. For example, it takes less self-control to stop physical touching under the clothes than it does to stop sexual involvement.

- "We've been dating for years."

Studies show that the earlier children begin dating alone, the greater the chance they will become sexually involved prior to high school graduation. In one study, 91% of the kids who began dating at age 12 had sex before graduation; 56% of those who began dating at age 13; 53% of those who began dating at age 14; 40% of those who began dating at age 15; and only 20% of those who began dating at age 16.[1]

Going out alone together is exciting for boys and girls. Developing relationships is exciting. But exploring the physical side of intimacy is the most pleasurable experience and provides the most immediate satisfaction. Therefore, the more time that younger kids are allowed to spend alone together, the further they will go in their physical exploration simply because of the cumulative time factor.

- "That's how we were made."

"If we weren't supposed to enjoy sex, why did God make us sexual beings?" It's a common question from teenagers.

For a lot of teens, sex is simply a natural choice. They haven't thought through and accepted the reasons to wait for sexual involvement. God did make us sexual beings and gave us the ability to enjoy sexual involvement. Having a sexual relationship is a natural biological function, but one we are expected to use with discipline and in the way God designed it.

You need to help your teens understand that many biological functions have rules attached to them. Burping is natural, but it is not usually acceptable to belch loudly without saying "Excuse me." Eating and sleeping are natural functions, but we don't eat or sleep whenever and wherever we please.

- "It's exciting."

Sex is exciting and pleasurable. Kids who have not learned self-discipline may not have the ability to say no to something pleasurable when the opportunity to enjoy it arises. Help your children develop self-discipline because it is the key to success in so many areas of life. *Doing right when you want to only takes energy. Doing right when you don't want to, takes self-discipline.* Teach your children the rewards of self-discipline and you will help them resist the pleasures of sex until they are in a marriage relationship.

- "It relaxes me."

Because orgasm releases sexual tension, it is true that intercourse can relax people. It serves as a stress reliever. In fact, it is a wonderful stress reliever. And kids who live under the pressures of trying to measure up to parental expectations, the need to get good grades and qualify for a scholarship, the peer pressures to conform, and the need to satisfy internal desires may choose sexual involvement to release some of that tension.

Teach your children to pursue other activities to relieve tension. While the effect may not be as fun as sexual involvement, many other physical activities can provide a physical stress release. Strenuous physical exercise, active sports, heavy physical chores, and even individual activities such as running, jogging, and swimming are wonderful physical stress relievers.

- "I want a child."

"Celeste, one of my students, is only 14," Wanda shared, "but she came into my classroom the other day and announced to me that she wanted a baby. I couldn't believe that she was serious, but as she talked, I realized that in her mind a baby would give her the sense of belonging she was missing in her family. She didn't care about quitting school, the financial challenges, or any of the other difficulties. She seemed determined to have a child in the next year."

Fortunately, most teens who are sexually active are not doing so to have children. They either hope and pray they don't conceive, or they take precautions to avoid pregnancy. However, it may shock you to learn that many teens feel a baby would complete their lives, fill a desperate need, or even give them the leverage to get a boyfriend to marry them or gain parental acceptance of a particular boy.

Teach your children early that babies are not toys to be used to get what they want. There are other ways to fill emotional and psychological needs. Children are a big responsibility, and children should not have children!

- "There's nothing wrong with having sex."

Most parents hope their children grow up with a healthy anticipation of a satisfying sexual relationship within a marriage relationship. Most would agree that there is nothing wrong with sex ... if you are married to your partner. However, some kids have not developed personal values about sex. For them, because they do not understand or accept God's standards, they honestly do not understand why adults consider premarital sex to be wrong.

To help your children develop their moral standards, focus on the next section of this chapter, which gives reasons to wait for a sexual relationship.

- "I don't want to lose my relationship."

"I didn't want to have sex," 15-year-old Cherise told her doctor, "but I love my boyfriend, and I didn't want to lose him. He said if I loved him, I would let him. So I did."

Giving into pressure from a partner is one of the oldest reasons or excuses for beginning a sexual relationship. Feeling one "owes" a date physical privileges is a wrong reason for having sex. Help your children develop the ability to say no to demands they are not ready to meet, especially in the area of physical intimacy.

- "I didn't mean to."

It is not uncommon for teens to become sexually involved without actually planning to do so. Drinking, taking drugs, being pressured by a dating partner or by friends, and having access to birth control (which removes most of the threat of an unwanted pregnancy) can contribute to a teen's sexual involvement. Then the responsibility is sometimes shrugged off with an "I didn't mean to" excuse after the fact.

Long before your teens begin dating, talk about these things. Help them see there are always choices they can make, even at the last minute. But choosing to say no earlier in the intimacy progression makes sticking to the refusal easier to do.

- "It makes me feel better inside."

The teen years are difficult. Your children are pulling away from dependency on you and working toward individual independence. There is a tension between wanting to belong to the family, to be cared for and protected, and the strong drive to become one's own person and make one's own choices.

Teens may feel left out when their families split up and their security is shattered. Teens may have abusive parents and desire love and acceptance without violence. Teens may feel that sex with different partners ensures popularity. In other words, sometimes teens use sex as an anesthetic or a pain killer for loneliness, for being afraid, for being unpopular with other teens.

Sex can temporarily make teens feel better. In the physical closeness, they may feel accepted, a sense of belonging, the warmth of intimacy, and an affirmation of self. The problem is, the feeling is temporary.

Help your teens develop inner strength and self-esteem. Help them understand intimacy and make the transition from dependence to independence.

- "It proves I'm grown up."

For some teens, sex is a passage between childhood and adulthood. When kids feel they are mature enough to make their own decisions, choosing sexual involvement is one way they believe they can make others accept them as "adults." A variation on this argument says that a sexual relationship tests a couple's compatibility, and it's actually good preparation for marriage. Many teens believe that sex is acceptable if one is engaged. Underlying all these beliefs is the idea that choosing to have sex is an "adult" decision and making it proves maturity. For a few teens, sex is simply a deliberate rebellion against their parents' rules, guidelines, or values.

Your teens need to see that adulthood means taking responsibility for making good choices. A sexual relationship does not make one an adult.

No matter why teens decide to have sex or go along with the pressure to get sexually involved, you can have a positive impact. Share the many good reasons to refrain from sexual activity before marriage.

Reasons for Kids Not to Have Sex

"It seems as if there are more reasons for kids to have sex before marriage than we can give them not to!" one father confessed. "Once I've told them 'Don't do it because it's wrong,' what more do I say?

Actually, there are many more reasons to say no than there are to say yes. But you must think through these reasons and be ready to share them with your kids. Sexual relationships outside of marriage are wrong, not just because God says they are, although that should be reason enough to refrain.

When God designed and fearfully and wonderfully made us, it was a complete package. The physical, spiritual, emotional, and psychological parts of our beings are inexorably intertwined. There is no such thing as a purely physical sex act.

Who should know better than God what the consequences of our choices will be for us? When God places a clear warning label on the inappropriate use of sex, it is for our protection and not to inhibit our fun. It is there to ensure guilt-free enjoyment of sex in the future. Premarital and out-of-wedlock sexual experiences *will* be harmful to your emotional, psychological, physical, and spiritual health!

When and if your kids understand that God's prohibitions are for their protection and motivated by His intense love, the prospects for waiting for sexual intimacy are greatly increased.

Teens who engage in premarital sex:

- Risk contracting sexually transmitted diseases.

Some sexually transmitted diseases are incurable (herpes) and some are fatal (AIDS). Some are damaging (Chlamydia can cause infertility, as can untreated gonorrhea. Syphilis can cause brain damage, heart disease, paralysis, insanity, and even death). Only a few diseases used to be identified as sexually transmitted diseases, now there are almost 30.

Teens cannot know if their sexual partners are healthy. Teens may not even be aware that they have a disease, so asking a partner to be honest about the risks is not a solution. Sexual relations with more than one partner increases the risk of contracting a serious disease. There is no such thing as 100%-guaranteed "safe sex." The only way to ensure a sexually transmitted disease is not contracted is to refrain from having sex.

- Risk becoming pregnant.

Even the most reliable birth control device or

medication is not 100% foolproof, and pregnancy is always a risk. In the case of teens who do not practice birth control, the odds of becoming pregnant are high, especially with repeated sexual activity.

Premarital sex can result in an unwanted or unplanned pregnancy. The girl (or couple) must then face the responsibility of having a child. Some may consider an abortion. However, this compounds the problem by killing an unborn child and can result in long-lasting psychological and spiritual guilt and regret.

- Risk becoming addicted to sex.

Like many other behaviors, sex can become addicting. Sexual relations with more than one partner can be a second part of the addiction.

Sex is both exciting and pleasurable, but the physical release and pleasure is short-lived. When it is over, it is over. The tension builds back up and the desire for pleasure is again present. There is a drive, a need, a lust for another sexual encounter. Sexual intimacy in a good marriage relationship is only one part of the pleasure and relationship. When teens have sex, they wake up alone the next day and have no one to reach for. When a married couple has sex, they can snuggle all night, wake up together, share the day, and have the emotional assurance and affirmation of belonging to one another.

Teens do not have that additional dimension, and therefore, they can find themselves addicted to the sexual act. They long for it, dream of it, plan for it, and eagerly engage in it in the same way a drug addict reaches for a fix.

- Risk a break in fellowship with God.

Deliberately going against God's stated standards is sin. Continuing in sin breaks the close fellowship with God. The psalmist tells us that if we hide sin in our hearts, God will not hear our prayers (Ps. 66:18). While it is true that if we confess our sin, God is faithful and will forgive the sin (1 John 1:9), we are reminded by the apostle Paul not to continue in sin just so God's grace will abound (Rom. 6:1–2).

Sexual sin is a sin against our own bodies (1 Cor. 6:18), a sin against our partners for encouraging them to sin, and a sin against God for disobeying His instructions.

- Risk encouraging another to sin.

One of our responsibilities as Christians is to help our weaker brothers or sisters in Christ and not to cause them to slip or fall (Rom. 14:12–16). By standing firm and refusing to commit sexual sin, the strong partner is helping the other remain true to God's standards, at least in that specific instance.

Giving in to their own lustful desires causes teens to encourage their partners to commit sexual sin.

- Risk experiencing guilt.

One consequence of going against one's convictions is living with depressing guilt, which can be defeating and discouraging. There may be guilt about not living up to God's expectations, parental expectations, personal standards, moral codes, or about not making the right choice.

For some teens, the guilt is overwhelming. The pain of guilt is not only emotional and psychological, but spiritual as well. There may also be physical pain as their bodies respond to the stress of guilt.

- Risk being in a relationship based on performance.

When unmarried partners, particularly young people, are involved in a sexual relationship there is a danger that the relationship will be based on performance. Acceptance is based on doing what is wanted. When the partner says no, the relationship may break up.

Kids who have sexual experiences with more than one partner prior to marriage often compare their partners' performances, including that of their spouse. This is an unfair and unproductive behavior.

When relationships are based on performance, the partners are accepted and loved for what they *do*, not who they *are*. This devalues the people involved.

- Risk more pain when relationships break up.

Breaking off a relationship is never simple and easy. It is usually painful, not only for the one being left but for the one who initiates the break up. An intimate physical relationship includes additional emotional and psychological ties, which cause additional pain when the relationship ends.

- Risk misinterpreting feelings.

Sexual intimacy intensifies feelings toward the partner. Sometimes these feelings seem stronger than they are because of the intensity of the emotional response to sex. Teens can misinterpret lust and physical attraction for love. They can believe that their addiction to another person is a result of love and not their sexual experiences. They can mistakenly read "love" into all the emotional responses they have for a partner.

- Risk a loss of self-esteem.

Some teens participate in sex because they believe that they cannot be loved for themselves, they are incapable of intimacy, they are not popular, or they won't be noticed by anyone in any other way. They try sex to increase their self-esteem.

However, when teens have sex to gain affirmation or acceptance, they secretly believe that without participating in sex, they will not be accepted. In reality, teens experience a loss in self-esteem while attempting to increase it.

- Risk God's judgment.

God pulls no punches. Sexual immorality, which includes premarital sex, is a sin, and it will be punished (1 Cor. 6:13–20; 7:1–5; Eph. 5:3; 1 Thess. 4:3–6). If teens participate in sexual relations and do not repent, they turn their backs on God. But God sent His Son to die for all sins, including sexual immorality (1 John 1:7). Even if your teens have sex, they have forgiveness if they repent of their sins. But Jesus also commands, "Go now and leave your life of sin" (John 8:11).

- Risk developing a bad reputation.

Despite the pressures to participate in sexual activity, there still exists a standard of moral purity that is valued. This is particularly true for girls. The old adage "good girls don't" is the popular belief that creates the paradox. Teens who are sexually active can develop a negative reputation for being lax, not only in sexual morals but also other morals.

- Risk not being able to appreciate the special experience of sharing one's first time with one's spouse.

Couples who had premarital sex often admit they wish they had waited until after marriage even though their first sexual experience was with each other. It is a unique experience to be able to give your spouse the gift of your virginity.

- Risk the inability to develop patience and self-control.

Two manifestations of the fruit of the Spirit in our lives are patience and self-control (Gal. 5:22–23). Teens who give into sexual temptation fail to develop these two essential qualities in their sexual life.

- Risk the inability to develop trust in the relationship.

Teens begin to build trust with their partners as they wait to satisfy their sexual desires. Insistence on sexual fulfillment may imply that if the partner says no, the relationship may dissolve. Teens who give in because of the possible loss of the relationship have no reason to trust or believe in their partner or expect the relationship to last or include love. Those who do not exhibit appropriate self-control or concern may raise questions about fidelity in the minds of their partners.

Help your teens in the decision-making process by helping them understand these important reasons to say no. Provide support for your teens by enforcing your dating rules and by living according to God's moral code in your own life. Then your teens will have a better chance to stand firm and be examples of believers who want God's best in their lives.

When Kids Don't Wait

Jackee and Sean let their dating get out of control, and they found themselves involved sexually. It was several months before they became so uncomfortable that they decided to break off the sexual involvement. They talked with their youth pastor at church.

"There's no way to go back and become virgins again," Jackee complained sadly. "I just want it to have never happened."

"Me too," Sean agreed.

The young pastor, pleased to see their genuine repentance, gave them good counsel. "No, you can't regain your physical virginity. But you can confess your sins and obtain forgiveness, not only from God, but from each other and from yourselves. Then you can plan your relationship to avoid situations in which you are tempted to become sexually involved again. It won't be easy. Few couples successfully break off a sexual relationship and maintain a close dating relationship. They become uncomfortable together without the sex. I applaud you for continuing in the relationship together. I wish you success."

If you discover that your teens are sexually active, it may be hard to accept. You may feel as if you have failed to communicate your values. Then you may become angry that your kids would let you down or that they made harmful choices for their lives. You may be uncomfortable and unsure of how to discuss the issues with your kids. This is one time you need to overcome your discomfort and confront the situation directly, firmly, and appropriately.

Exactly how you handle the situation will

depend on what you discover your kids have done, and at what point your discovery occurs.

Wendy walked into her son's bedroom and found him and his girlfriend having sex. "Stop that this minute!" Wendy screamed. She grabbed her son by the arm and literally pulled him off the bed, yelling at him all the while. The girl cowered as far away from Wendy as she could get, her eyes as big as saucers as she held the sheet up to her chin to hide her nakedness.

"Get dressed and get into the living room. NOW!" Wendy demanded.

The next hour was traumatic for both Wendy and the kids. Wendy left little doubt about how she felt about what they had been doing, their morals, their character, or any future activities that would not be tolerated in the house.

Wendy's anger was understandable. Her approach to stopping the situation may have been effective. But to ensure any long-range, lasting changes in the kids' behavior, Wendy needs to do more than yell and forbid them to have sex.

Not too many parents actually catch their kids in the act of having sex. Those who do often respond as Wendy did. More often than not, parents discover their teens are sexually active when a pregnancy occurs, when they overhear conversations, or when they find birth control devices in their kids' rooms. Sometimes parents are sensitive enough to their teens that they notice the signs of physical involvement.

Will noticed his son had started studying in his room for long hours, and then he had his girlfriend come over and study with him. Will became suspicious and put the boy's room off limits for the couple.

Margaret noticed that her son, Charles, was spending more and more time at his girlfriend's house after school. When Margaret discovered that his girlfriend's mother had started working and the kids were home alone, Margaret insisted that they meet at her house instead.

If you suspect your teen is considering sexual involvement (i.e., you find condoms in your son's room) or if you suspect sexual involvement has already begun, confront your teen. Remember your role in a confrontation is not to make your child defensive or angry but to change the behavior you consider unacceptable. Do your best to remain calm. You cannot choose for your teen, nor can you change what has already happened. All you can hope to do is prevent future sexual involvement.

Tell your teen what you have observed, found, or overheard. Explain the conclusions you have drawn. Explain how you feel. Ask your teen to discuss the level of involvement he or she has engaged in and how to prevent further sexual activity.

If your teen admits to sexual activity, help him or her to see that activity as a sin and lead your child to repentance. Then talk with your child's partner and have a similar conversation. As you discuss the issue, read 1 John 1:6–2:6 together. Talk about how sin keeps us from fellowship with others and with the Lord Jesus Christ. Invite them to seek God's forgiveness together and to ask God to give them the self-control to be obedient in the area of sexual purity.

It is not enough to stop there. Help your kids identify what roadblocks they need to set up in order not to take the same detour again. What steps of accountability should be put into place? What activities and locations should they avoid? Which friends should they avoid? What time limits should be imposed? Who will your kids call if they are afraid they are getting into trouble?

It is important that you set the tone of this discussion. While you do not need to hide your hurt and disappointment, you need to deal with your anger before you deal with your kids. Maintain enough control during the conversation so you will not alienate your kids or put them on the defensive so they won't discuss the issues. Changes in behavior won't occur just because they were discovered. Your kids have to choose to change and accept help in following through on the promises they make to themselves, to one another, and to God.

Notes
1. Jeannie Echenique, "Early Dating May Lead to Early Sex," *USA Today*, 12 November 1986, D1.

8

WHAT IS
THE GOAL
OF DATING?

Estelle told me she was planning to get married for the fourth time. Because she had been divorced for about a year and hadn't dated anyone seriously, I questioned her about whom she was planning to marry. It was a guy she had met only a month before. I tried to hide my shock.

"I don't date men," she confessed sheepishly. "I just marry them."

Therein lies the problem, Estelle.

Dating Is for Learning about Relationships

Casual dating, going out with different members of the opposite sex at different times, helps kids learn about relating to the opposite sex on a casual, non-committed basis. Young people automatically relate differently to one another on a date than they do at other times they may be together. Consider the difference between a boy taking a girl to the movies, buying popcorn, and sharing it and the same two kids accidently meeting at the movies, sitting together, and sharing a bag of popcorn. There is a unique awareness of one another if being together has been planned as a date. On a date, girls often dress to impress and boys adopt grown-up manners. Both are aware that when they enter a room, they are viewed as a couple. There is often more consideration for each other on a date because partners want to discover and cater to each other's preferences.

Young people date so they can explore relationships with the opposite sex that don't fall under the buddy or companion category. They date to reach an awareness of one another as members of the opposite sex. Dating helps teens learn selflessness as they put the likes and desires of their partners above their own.

Teens do not get to know one another by exchanging personal information sheets, so they need time to talk, observe, share, participate with, and learn about one another. Teens need to see one another in a variety of settings so they can observe and experience responses. Over time, they see how others respond emotionally to frustration, success, setbacks, illness, good fortune, and different people. During this process, teens ask the question "Is this the type of person I want to be around?" If the answer is yes, then that person is included in the dating circle. If the answer is no, that person is eliminated as a dating partner.

As teens learn about others, they gain insight about themselves. They see what types of people they attract and what types please them. Teens get feedback as others respond to their behaviors. They may choose to make changes to be more acceptable within their peer group.

Dating different young people is a rite of passage necessary for teens in their developmental process. Dating helps them learn about others and themselves in a unique way.

Dating Is for Exploring One Special Relationship

As young people discover that they have more fun with or are attracted to one of their dates more than the others, they begin to focus on that partner. They may want to go steady. As they single out that one person, a curiosity to get to know that person better usually develops. Dating now becomes a way to increase the intimacy between the couple.

Just as dating changes the relationship between two young people who have grown up together as friends, dating one person exclusively changes the relationship. When a commitment is made to date only one partner, a sense of uniqueness is added to the relationship. Partners agree that certain prerogatives go along with the promise of exclusivity. The sense of belonging intensifies and the desire to get to know one another increases.

Through the process of dating one another, a couple evaluates their compatibility. Behaviors, responses, and choices are considered, not only in relationship to self but to the other. Kids begin to learn both the freedom and the limitations involved in making a commitment to just one other person. Then they can evaluate whether they are ready to live with those limits.

Going steady increases the time spent alone as a couple because most free time and all of the dating time is spent with that special someone. Therefore, the relationship can deepen. It can also break up if the partners discover that they are not happy spending so much time together.

Chad loved Carla, he thought. Before he and Carla started dating exclusively, Chad found himself comparing all the other girls to Carla, and they didn't measure up. He was sure he wanted to marry Carla as soon as he was old enough. He knew he only wanted to go out with Carla, and Carla agreed. So they made a commitment. Soon Chad was bored. He discovered Carla was cute, funny, fun, and made him laugh, but she didn't like to talk about anything serious. She didn't seem to have any ambitions, goals, or spiritual commitment. Chad wanted more.

Through the dating process, young people learn that first attractions may not be enough to sustain a relationship. Compatibility on several levels is necessary for a relationship to develop depth and strength. Chad promised himself not to be fooled in the future by first impressions. He realized he would need to date someone for several months in order to carefully explore the different aspects of their relationship.

Remember Estelle from the beginning of the chapter? She has not learned that dating helps explore a special relationship to discover if it can last. Therefore, Estelle has gone through three divorces and may be headed for more.

Dating Myths

A group of parents was asked what dating myths they had to give up when their kids started dating. Most admitted that there were some misconceptions they had cherished.

- "I know what it is like. I was young once myself."

The world changes faster and faster. Dating today is very different than it was when you were young. It is vastly different than when your parents were teens. In the early 60s, the big question was "Do you kiss good-bye on the first date?" The question today may be whether to have sex, whether to drink, or whether to do drugs.

In most contemporary families, both parents work. This leaves the homes open for teens to meet and spend time alone unsupervised. As the number of latchkey kids, and parents who work more than one job, increases, so does the number of kids left home alone in the evenings. The ability to be alone together increases the opportunity to explore physical intimacy or provides the opportunity for kids' convictions to be tested.

Peer pressure to make inappropriate choices is strong because our society has accepted these choices as the norm. Even having a baby out of wedlock no longer carries the public stigma it used to. A recent newspaper article claimed that 30% of all babies born in the United States today are born out of wedlock. Instead of shame, many young girls are proud of their pregnancies.

Today teens in many states can obtain birth control pills or devices without consent or the knowledge of their parents. Even the availability of abortions on demand may allow some teens to participate in sexual activity because an unwanted pregnancy can be "taken care of."

Dating relationships and choices are very different than they were when you were dating.

- "They're too young for me to worry."

Are kids ever too young for you not to worry about two members of the opposite sex spending long hours alone together?

Angela was cleaning her son Joshua's closet and found a letter addressed to him. There were nude Polaroids of a young girl and a letter written to Joshua. It suggested that the girl could come over one day after school so they could "have fun together." Joshua was 10 years old.

- "Broken hearts mend quickly when kids are young."

Not necessarily. Broken hearts do mend, as most of us have discovered, but the pain of rejection is as real to a 14-year-old as it is to a 29-year-old. Just because your 14-year-old is not ready to make a life-long commitment, in your best judgment, do not discount the very real pain involved in the break up of a serious relationship.

- "Starting over in a new relationship means starting over."

Laura was secretly glad when Danny broke off his relationship with Jolene. She felt they were getting too physical with each other. Laura had often entered the living room to find them on the couch, locked in each other's embrace, and kissing, oblivious to the rest of the world. Despite her urging to watch television, go outside for a walk, or get involved in other activities, the kids inevitably returned to their kissing and hugging as soon as possible.

Laura was sure that there would be a little breathing room in her worrying now that Danny would be dating someone else. Surely it would take time to develop a new relationship to

141

the point where kissing and hugging on the couch was the only desired activity.

Wrong! Laura didn't realize there is a tendency to start the next relationship about where the last one left off. Although there is a short period of escalation in the relationship to get it to the point where the last one was, that delay is usually very brief. Sure enough, within a couple weeks, Danny was on the couch, kissing and hugging his new steady girlfriend, Gloria.

- "If my teens are good and make the 'right' choices, their dating partners will be glad and will appreciate this."

Leonard was surprised when his son, Willy, told him that Trina had broken up with him because he was "too good." Willy didn't want to get too involved physically. Apparently Trina was used to more and wanted more. Willy was upset because it seemed that making the right choice cost him what he wanted most, Trina. He even questioned the wisdom of his choice.

Leonard reassured Willy that a girl who did not agree with his right choices was not the right one for him in a long-term relationship. It was still a long time before Willy was convinced of that.

It's important to teach your teens to make choices consistent with biblical principles, but you also must let them know that they won't always be popular because of those choices. They may even be rejected because they are doing the right things.

- "Now that they are dating, they are growing up and will be out of the house soon."

"I'll admit that I saw Darryl's steady relationship as the beginning of the end. I thought that within a couple years he would get married and be out on his own. I had mentally converted his bedroom into a den. That was five years ago, and Darryl is still home."

Young people are starting to date at younger ages, and they're getting involved with serious relationships in their late teens. But they are waiting later to get married. It is not uncommon for men and women in their late 20s to still live at home. They may even have left home to live on their own only to return to live with their parents.

What myths have you cherished and not examined in the light of your kids' current reality? Write down your ideas. Discuss them with your teens and see what feedback you receive. You could be surprised. You may need to release or revise some of your favorite myths!

Dating is more than a romantic relationship. Dating is more than a sexually charged relationship. Dating is a process through which kids learn about one another, adult relationships, themselves, and the consequences and rewards of commitment.

Help your kids make the most of their dating experiences. Make the learning fun and insightful. Help them make dating a wholesome and healthy process.

APPENDIX

Selected Bibliography

Ameiss, Bill, and Jane Graver. *Love, Sex, and God (ages 14 and up)*. Vol. 5. *Learning about Sex: A Series for the Christian Family*. St. Louis: Concordia, 1995.

Bell, Ruth. *Changing Bodies, Changing Lives: A Book for Teens on Sex and Relationships*. New York: Random House, 1989.

Bimler, Richard. *Sex and the New You (ages 11–14)*. Vol. 4. *Learning about Sex: A Series for the Christian Family*. St. Louis: Concordia, 1995.

Buth, Lenore. *How to Talk Confidently with Your Child about Sex and Appreciate Your Own Sexuality Too*. Vol. 6. *Learning about Sex: A Series for the Christian Family*. St. Louis: Concordia, 1995.

Dobson, James. *Emotions: Can You Trust Them?* Ventura: Regal Books, 1980.

Kirby, Scott. *Dating: Guidelines from the Bible*. Grand Rapids: Baker Book House, 1979.

McDowell, Josh. *The Secret of Loving*. Wheaton: Tyndale, 1985.

McDowell, Josh, and Dick Day. *Why Wait? What You Need to Know about the Teen Sexuality Crisis*. San Bernardino: Here's Life, 1987.

McDowell, Josh, and Paul Lewis. *Givers, Takers, and Other Kinds of Lovers*. Wheaton: Tyndale, 1981.

Mylander, Charles. *Running the Red Lights*. Ventura: Regal Books, 1986.

Nonkin, Leslie J. *I Wish My Parents Understood*. New York: Freundlich Books, 1982.

Reed, Bobbie. *Single Mothers Raising Sons*. Nashville: Thomas Nelson, 1988.

Stedman, Rick. *Pure Joy*. Chicago: Moody Press, 1993.

Talley, Jim A., and Bobbie Reed. *Too Close Too Soon*. Nashville: Thomas Nelson, 1982.

Wright, Norman, and Marvin Inmon. *A Guidebook to Dating, Waiting, and Choosing a Mate*. Eugene: Harvest House, 1978.